BRING HIM
HOME

BRING HIM HOME

A TWIN FLAME LOVE STORY

MIGUEL DEAN

Sacred Stories
PUBLISHING

Bring Him Home: A Twin Flame Love Story
Miguel Dean

Tradepaper ISBN: 978-1-945026-54-6
Electronic ISBN: 978-1-945026-55-3

Library of Congress Control Number: 2019939506

Editor: Evan J. Corey
Cover Design: Mikaela San Pietro

Published by Sacred Stories Publishing
Printed in the United States of America

May the energy of this story be a catalyst for
healing the deep wounds between men and women.
May we have the courage to look inside ourselves and do our
work so that we may realise the divine twin flame union within.
May we learn to father and mother ourselves and take care of our inner child.
May we remember what it is to love ourselves, each other,
all sentient beings and this sacred earth, for ourselves,
our children, and the generations to come.

PROLOGUE

It wasn't so much that he noticed her when she entered the room, rather, he noticed how everything else seemed to fade; like a camera, zoomed and focused in on the subject of the photograph, everything else was a blur. The moving shapes of the other people were only vaguely apparent amongst the distant sounds and bustle at the author fair where he was promoting himself and his books.

Her blonde hair was like a glowing beacon, and she walked with the gentle grace of a quietly confident woman who knows that she is pleasing to the eye. He couldn't tell her age from where he stood, although the way she moved suggested that she was not young and had experienced a generous portion of life.

A voice in front of him returned him to his location in the room, and he focused on his author's role as people came and went from the table which he stood behind, littered with piles of books. Sometimes a person would pause and engage him in conversation while others just browsed, leafing through the pages. Occasionally, he would sign a copy for a customer. All the while, he was aware that she was still in the room, making her way slowly round to where he stood.

He hoped that she would hurry up so he could engage her in conversation, but the time arrived for him to give his presentation. He made his way from behind the stand and walked through the crowds of dawdling browsers to the room where he needed to be. He readied himself at the front of the small hall with a sip of water and a glance at his notes. A steady stream of people arrived unhurriedly in ones, twos, and threes and he waited as the chairs filled, and the clock silently moved its hands. Then, at the last minute, she arrived, settling herself into an empty seat at the back of the room. He felt unusually self-conscious by her presence, knowing that she had come to listen to what he had to say. He brought his attention back to the moment as best as he could and took another sip of water before beginning to speak. He shared a little of his story and how his latest book had come to be written, doing his best not to look in her direction, though he was acutely aware that she sat motionlessly and listened with a calm smile across her pretty face.

Time always accelerated when he gave a talk and soon he was back behind his table with his books. There was the usual flurry of interest to buy a book that often followed his heartfelt speaking, and he engaged appreciatively with the people that came to buy, to ask questions or who just wanted to share their stories with him.

His passions were to make a difference to the world through his writing and his own inner journey of self-actualisation. Intensely aware of the suffering and injustice in the world, he had pledged his life to create a more beautiful world for the children and generations to come. Events like these helped remind him that he did have a positive impact on people's lives.

He forgot her for a moment, until she arrived at his stand before him, smiling. She had an otherworldly, angelic quality about her, and it was her eyes that he immediately found most alluring. They were blue, clear and bright. When she smiled the gentle squint seemed to intensify the radiance of the sparkling beam that emanated from them.

He glanced down at her elegant fingers to see that there was no wedding ring. It was an almost automatic thing to do; though he was also without a ring, he was not available. He was trying hopelessly to salvage a five-year relationship. His heart still belonged to another and, even though he didn't want to accept it, the writing was on the wall, and the outcome was inevitable. It was just a matter of time. Although he had always been faithful, at this moment, as this strange, beautiful woman stood before him, unexpected feelings arose, and he blushed inwardly as if he were guilty of infidelity and that she might be able to read his mind.

As he spoke, his words seemed to have lost their usual flow, and he felt awkward and clumsy; gone was his usual eloquence. He retreated into a mock confidence that sometimes emerged when he was nervous. In their conversation, she revealed that she had been travelling abroad for over a year and on returning home she was aware of the need to find other like-minded souls now that she felt so different to when she had left. She asked him if he was a member of any personal development or holistic growth groups that might be of value to her in making connections. He didn't, and his arrogance surfaced a little when he suggested that she look inside of her self for that which she was seeking. He didn't have much time for the New Age movement, preferring to call it the 'New Cage'! In his haste to share his opinion and, possibly because he was not yet single, he failed to see that she may have also wanted to attend a meeting so that she could see him again.

The conversation lost its flow at this point and, glancing around, she noticed other people waiting patiently to talk with him; all too quickly she politely excused herself. He didn't want her to go. He tried to find something witty or memorable to say, but all that he could manage was an awkward smile. He breathed a small sigh as he watched her walk away, acutely aware of the gorgeous curves in her tight-fitting jeans. He exhaled once again, this time more heavily and, returning his attention to the people in front of him, she fell from his mind.

CHAPTER 1

I t was nine months before he was to see her again.

He wasn't supposed to be on an internet dating site, but he was. His relationship had wound its inevitable way to the end seven months earlier and, he had left his home once again with his broken open heart. He didn't believe in broken hearts; the pain he felt, as well as the grief of leaving his partner, was also a purging of old pain from childhood wounds. He preferred to consider the discomfort as growing pains, or the breaking open of his heart like the petals of a rose. And he knew that he needed time to heal, time to let the woman who he had loved so much, go. He was surprised at how deeply he had allowed her inside him. He thought that the final months of disharmony would have played some part in making the end a little easier, but this was not to be.

We can prepare for an ending in our minds as much as we like. But when it actually comes to pass, the grief of the physical parting is often not reduced by the awareness of its coming and is still extremely painful. The end of this relationship was particularly hard because as well as leaving his lover, he also needed to leave his home; she owned the house where they had lived. When he finally decided to give in to the inevitable truth that the relationship was unsalvageable, he plucked up the courage to leave and began his search for a new home.

Before long he moved into the house of another woman who he had recently met. They both knew that he was still grieving the end of his relationship and was on the rebound, but he needed somewhere to stay, and his confidence had suffered from the failure of his relationship. He would need to increase his income now that he was not sharing living costs with his ex-partner and living with another person made sense financially. They knew that his moving in so quickly after meeting was a gamble but hoped that the passing of time would heal his heart and they might fall in love. But it never happened. As the weeks passed his heart did indeed heal, but he could feel no love for his new companion. After five months they decided that it was best for them to go their separate ways.

He moved into a friend's spare room until he got back on his feet and could find somewhere more suitable to live. Each day he would spend time feeling the fullness of his loneliness, but it didn't seem to get any easier. Life somehow felt incomplete on his own, and he felt, for the most part, that he was just going through the motions of living as he drifted around a joyless, grey world. Though those feelings were strong, he also felt a growing desire for connection, companionship, sex, and intimacy. He knew he needed time to heal from all he had been through and that time alone was a good idea; he tried to remind himself that the intimacy that he sought with a woman was also the intimacy that he needed to find within himself. His outward desire was a distraction from his need to feel and fully grieve an old wound so that he might be able to then deepen his connection with the divine feminine within himself that had been so suddenly torn from him in his infancy. He knew that although there was a longing in his heart to be with another, part of what he felt was an uncomfortableness at being fully with himself.

He had lost his mother to cancer when he was a baby, and the abrupt loss of the woman who was the embodiment of love and the feminine had wounded him deeply. He knew that his journey to healing, lay not in finding a lover to become the surrogate mother for his inner child, but in connecting and nurturing the divine feminine essence within his own heart. He had spent so much time searching externally for what could only be healed internally.

It had been seven months since he had left his five-year relationship. During that time, he had done his best to find answers and healing within himself. But on this dark and cold evening, alone in his room, before he was aware of what he was doing, he had signed up for the online dating site. He hurriedly created a brief profile of himself and added a few photos. The monthly subscription was paid, and he browsed through the images and profiles of the women that caught his attention. Initially, it wasn't so much that he thought he would contact any of the women; he just wanted to avoid the feeling of loneliness and allow his imagination to fast forward to a time when he might no longer be alone.

As his fingers guided the cursor across the pages, though, he felt a pang of shame, as if he was doing something wrong. Wasn't he supposed to be spending time alone? Didn't he need to do some inner healing work so that he was a little more complete unto himself? But, like an addict, his need for a hit of female company silenced his doubts, and he continued to browse the site.

Some of the women were pleasing to the eye, yet, on reading the information they had written about themselves, he felt it unlikely that they would have much in common. After all, he was a somewhat unconventional man, and he knew that many women would find him a little too weird! He didn't fit into the usual macho man stereotype. He didn't play or watch sport, he was not financially motivated, and he wasn't interested in status. Instead, he had adopted a unique masculine identity throughout his life, what he referred to as his sacred masculinity. Its divine strength was derived from the honouring, revering, and protecting of women, and a recognition of the sacredness of life.

He had found that some women were not necessarily accustomed to such a celebration of their femininity and he was quite aware that the kind of woman he wanted to share his life with was a rare creature and might not be easily found. He often imagined meeting 'the one.' But the more he thought about it, the more unlikely he felt that he was in the right place to find anyone compatible. Still, he carried on looking at the profiles anyway. As an afterthought, he reminded himself that if he did find a date, he would take his time, move slowly and be sure that even if he liked her a lot, he would not fall in love so quickly this time. The pain in his heart from his last experience was still too fresh.

Then, her photograph appeared before him. His eyes were held transfixed, initially at the simple beauty and kindness of her face. There wasn't an instant recognition, but the more he looked, the more there was something familiar about her. Her pose was playful and light as she sat looking at the camera. There was an innocent aura about her that gripped him. He thought she was probably out of his league. He scanned the words that she had written and her other photographs, and before he really knew what he was doing, he sent her a short message. He closed the laptop feeling a mixture of excitement, shame, and fear. But it was done. The message was sent, and now he would just have to be patient, even though waiting was not one of his strengths.

To his delight, the following evening when he opened his laptop and returned to the dating site, there was a message. It was from her. His sense of fear and shame were forgotten, and he immediately found himself surfing a wave of excitement. He answered the message, doing his best to disguise how delighted he was that she had responded. A little later in the evening, she replied again, and they wrote to each other a few more times before he decided to see if she was a potential date or whether she just wanted a pen pal. He stated plainly that he wasn't really a big fan of written communication and that he would prefer to have a conversation by phone if she was happy to give him her number. He knew that his mind would build up a picture of this attractive woman by filling in all the information about her that he did not yet know, which was pretty much everything, and he didn't want this to happen. He wanted to know her, the real person. Hearing her voice, the tone, the pitch, the cadence would give him more information in a few moments than pages of written messages. To his surprise, she felt the same. She gave him her telephone number, and as agreed, the following evening he called.

He dearly hoped that her voice was in alignment with the warm glow that he felt when he looked at her photographs. Sure enough, when she answered his call, her gentle voice pleased him and only complimented the visual image he had of her on the computer in front of him. She spoke calmly and assuredly, and they took turns asking questions to get to know each other a little, and she laughed easily at his light-hearted humour. After a momentary pause in the conversation, she asked if he had been at a book fair the previous year in April. When he acknowledged that he had, she asked whether he realised that they had met there. It wasn't often that he found himself lost for words and, embarrassed, he stammered something about how he had known that there was something familiar about her. She teased him a little, and he felt his cheeks glow, and he was grateful that she could not see his crimson blush. Yes, the woman with the golden blonde hair and the delicious curves! The welcome memory of her returned and, immediately, he was alerted to the synchronicity of them meeting again on the dating site. He was not able to be with her nine months earlier, but now he was single and available. Was it possible that they were meant to be together, but the timing had not been right before which was why they were meeting again now? He knew his mind was racing ahead, and he reminded himself that they hadn't even met yet! Still, when he looked at her photos on his computer screen, she looked even more gorgeous.

Forty minutes of easy flowing conversation passed in a flash, and they said goodnight, but not before they had arranged to meet the coming weekend at a pub halfway between where they each lived. He had asked her if he could see her without too much hope that she would accept, thinking that it was perhaps too soon, but he was both surprised and delighted when she had agreed to the suggestion. It appeared that she also wanted to know if there was an energy between them and was not frightened to meet. They decided that she would choose a pub and text him with the location. He didn't mind where they met; he was happy to drive pretty much anywhere to meet her.

Later that evening as he lay in bed reliving their conversation his mind began making mischief. What if she didn't like the fact that he had long hair? What if the world that she inhabited was too different from his? What if she didn't care about the things that were important to him? What if she wasn't attracted to him?

He decided that these fears were beyond his control and all he could do was turn up at the agreed time and place; the rest would be up to fate. Friday was only three days away, and he would soon know if this was the beginning or the end of something. He turned over on his side and tucked the bed covers tightly around himself. Eventually, his chattering mind settled, the excitement in his belly subsided, and he drifted off to sleep.

HE HAD TWO flats to view, emails to write and phone calls to make. All the while, the thought of meeting this new mysterious and beautiful woman was a constant distraction. The second flat that he visited was perfect, and he gratefully busied himself over the next few days moving in and getting himself settled.

Friday finally came only to find that when he turned the car lights on something was not right. The side lights were working, and when he put them on the main beam they worked, but when he dipped them there was only blackness. It was getting late by now, and there would be no shops or garages open; even if he did find somewhere, it would probably mean he would be late for their meeting. He didn't fancy his chances at fitting new bulbs, even if he could find somewhere to buy them, as he had no tools and was not great when it came to practical tasks.

He had been so looking forward to meeting her that he just couldn't cancel at this late stage. There was only one thing for it. He adjusted the setting on the main beam so that the lights were facing down onto the road as much as possible and, apologising in advance to any oncoming motorists that he might dazzle, he set off. He wondered if the faulty car lights were an omen, a sign that he was not meant to meet her. Was this divine intervention warning him? But his anticipation was much too strong, and he dismissed the thoughts as best he could.

To his relief, nobody flashed him to tell him to dip his headlights as he wound his way along the main roads. By the time he was on the motorway, his concern had disappeared and been replaced with excited anticipation at meeting her.

He arrived early at the pub and parked in the corner of the dark car park where he sat for a moment, drinking in the silence and enjoying the obscurity of the night. He felt more alive than he had in a long time. On entering the pub, he went to the bar and bought himself half a pint of lager. He didn't drink alcohol very often, and he hoped that just a little would settle his nerves. He took his drink and sat down. But there were too many other tables close by, and he picked up his drink and moved to one by the door where he would be able to see her arrive. This new location would also give them more privacy to talk without being overheard.

He waited anxiously in the noisy room, fully aware that it was possible that she might not even come. There were too many people, particularly too many men, and he was reminded of how different he was to other men. He found that he had always related better to women, probably because he was more in tune with his feminine side. His sensitive nature found little common ground with most men, and he was particularly distressed by the way most men objectified women. As he observed the bustle of the bar, he wondered if the lack of a feminine presence in his childhood had given him his deep reverence and respect for women.

The door opened every so often to let someone in, but each time it was not her. After what seemed like an eternity, she arrived. He was not disappointed at what he saw. Memories of her and the magnetic attraction that he had felt at their meeting the previous year came flooding back. His face broke into a massive smile as his eyes drunk in the beauty of the woman that stood before him. He took her outstretched hand which was probably extended for him to shake; instead, he pulled himself towards her a little and kissed her lightly on the cheek. She smelt exquisite.

She wore a blue denim jacket and jeans, with a pretty blouse, a brightly coloured pashmina draped around her shoulders and smart black ankle boots with a small heel. She looked amazing. He went to the bar and ordered her vodka and tonic and returned to sit across the table from her.

As the conversation ebbed and flowed between them, he tried to keep his eyes on hers, even though he wanted to look her up and down and inspect every aspect of her form. It always felt to him that on a first date each person should be allowed to stand up and turn around slowly so that the physical form could be seen and appreciated fully. In this way, it would then be easier to focus more fully on the conversation instead of being distracted by trying to sneak glances at the physical features. He thought that perhaps it was just a man thing, or maybe it was just him! He wondered what she thought about him and tried to guess from her conversation and body language, but he knew he was not really in a fit state to assess anything objectively. He felt unusually excited and probably looked like a Cheshire cat grinning ridiculously from ear to ear!

Before long he had to excuse himself and visit the toilet. He cursed his body for causing him to miss some precious minutes with her and half an hour later, to his dismay, he needed to go again. He didn't know if it was the alcohol or the emotions that were affecting his bladder. Then, to make matters worse, his nose began to run, as if he was experiencing some sort of allergic reaction. What was going on? He wished that his body would behave itself; he so wanted to be at his best.

After a while she asked him the question that he knew could make or break her willingness to see him again.

"How long have you been single?"

He knew he had to be honest, telling the truth was important to him. If he were to have the opportunity to possibly have a relationship with this woman he would have to begin from an honest, true place. He told her what had happened since they had last met at the book fair, watching carefully to gauge her reaction. But she said little in response to his story and their conversation quickly wound itself round to more comfortable topics.

They talked about some humorous experiences of online dating and, judging by some of her encounters, he at least had to be in the 'relatively okay' category. All the while his nose kept running, and he kept self-consciously blowing it, acutely aware that it was probably looking rather red by now!

He bought another drink for them both and was glad that she was not hurrying away, yet the evening was passing too quickly. He wished that he had the power to pause time, but this was not currently one of the skills that he had.

Not long before the pub was due to close, she excused herself to use the bathroom. He waited until she was almost out of sight before turning to admire the view of her womanly curves as she left the bar and he whispered a little prayer that he might, one day, be blessed enough to lie naked with her. All too soon the time arrived for them to part, and he walked her to her car. The only good thing about their parting was the invigorating cold night air and the privacy granted by the dark where they were alone together for the first time. He wanted to know if he would ever see her again. He wanted to write a date in his diary that was clear and visible that he could look at time and time again so that he would know she was real. Still, he knew that her promise to call him was the best that he could hope for. She would probably need time to decide, especially after his confession that he had not been technically single for very long at all.

Why didn't he need time? Yes, he found her very attractive, but he had met many good-looking women and had not felt the same level of attraction; there was something else that whispered to him of the importance of being with her. Their slightly awkward parting embrace lasted only a moment, but it was long enough to feel the softness of woman against him, for him to inhale a breath of her delicate fragrance. He wanted more.

He walked back to his car, climbed in and sat for a moment, watching her drive away. Then he turned the keys in the ignition, cursed his faulty headlights, made a mental note to get them fixed the next day and drove himself home.

A COUPLE OF days passed, but he heard nothing and thoughts of her dominated his mind. Would she agree to see him again?

He tried to remind himself that if it were meant to be then, it would be, but it was a futile attempt to find peace. Any vague thoughts that he had of a solitary life were gone, and he knew that he wanted to see her again; he wanted to be with her.

At first, he accepted that there was nothing he could do apart from practice patience, but on the third evening, struggling with his sense of powerlessness, he changed his mind and decided to write. He messaged her and asked for her email address and sat down to write. In his letter, he told her of his strong feelings for her and how he knew that it didn't look good on paper that he had spent so little time alone. He reminded her that he had not been in love for many months and, although he had been living with a woman until recently, he had not loved her, it had been more of a mutually convenient situation. He continued saying how he knew seeing him again was a risk, but that he believed that living fully was all about risk. If they did not meet again and explore a relationship, they would never know how compatible they might be. He asked her to listen to the voice of her heart and not just her mind. He didn't want to influence her decision, but at the same time, for his own peace of mind, he needed to know that he had expressed his thoughts and feelings. Whatever came to pass he would know that he had done everything that he could to see her again. He hit the send button on his computer and sat back in his chair, resigned to his fate of more waiting.

That evening, he chanced upon a poem that warned of the amazing things that might happen if you fell in love with a conscious man. There was the potential for an amazing depth of love and beauty and also the potential for great healing which might not always be comfortable. The poem seemed to sum up his feelings so clearly that he decided to send this to her, too. She might find the poem too weird and he knew sending it was also a risk. However, he wanted to be honest with her so that she would know the sort of man he was, as the poem seemed to be about him.

The wait was delightfully short-lived; a few hours later she replied to his email, saying that she would like to see him again. She mentioned how much she loved poetry and on reading the words she had felt a tingling sensation all over her body. He noticed the date in the bottom corner of his laptop. Until that moment he had been unaware that it was February 14th, St. Valentine's Day!

CHAPTER 2

Before long they were together again in a quiet pub in the countryside. He bought their drinks despite her offer to pay. He would not hear of it and joked that he would pay for the drinks and she could get the bill when they went out for something to eat. They found a cosy corner to sit, and she did most of the talking. He loved the sound of her voice. While he listened, he was able to admire her beauty, but their time together was cut short; unbeknownst to them the pub only stayed open for the lunchtime trade. The weather outside was cold and windy; nevertheless, they took a short walk along the path and up the small hill behind the car park. The chilly gusts buffeted them, and her nose began to run and turn red, her eyes watered and her usually tidy hair was soon wild and unkempt. He enjoyed seeing her in this new light with the wildness of the weather and her elegance enhanced by the bleak, wintry countryside that framed her as they walked side by side.

He wanted so much to take her hand in his, but he wasn't sure whether it would be moving too quickly for her. They talked about this and that, but mostly she talked, and he listened. He enjoyed hearing the easy, gentle, feminine lilt of her voice and he wanted to know her, he wanted to know all about her. She told him that she owned a small café that she ran. Her lovely smile broadened across her beautiful face as she told of how it was a place of safety and warmth, where all the food and drinks were prepared and served with love and kindness. He was impressed by her generous and magnanimous spirit; he could see that she was a kind soul.

She told him of her passion for books, literature, and culture and his heart sank a little. Even though he was an author, he was not really a very cultured man. He made a mental note of what was important to her and decided there and then that he was more than willing to be introduced to her world. In the past, he was aware that he had been too closed and set in his ways and he had pledged to himself that he would be more open to whatever life brought his way. It was time that he discovered and appreciated a little more of what culture had to offer

The conversation wound its way along with the path around the hill, and she talked about her part-time studies at university. He felt a pang of sadness, wondering if she would have time for him, but he let go of the thought and brought his attention back to her enthusiasm as she told him about her studies. As he listened, they made their way back to where their cars were parked. His little blue Peugeot and her little green Citroen were parked side by side as if keeping each other company while they waited for their owners' return.

He stood in front of her and took her gloved hands in his and looked for a moment into her pretty blue eyes. She held his gaze with only a hint of shyness, and he asked if he could kiss her. She said nothing but kept looking at him with smiling eyes, so he took a small step, slowly leaned forward and kissed her gently on her mouth. There was no sign of yielding from her fragile, cool lips and in a moment he had pulled back. They looked at each other again, this time with blushing smiles.

"That tickled," she said, giggling. "I have never kissed a man with a beard before."

He apologised with a grin and added "You may find it will tickle less if you open your mouth."

She quickly changed the subject, and they agreed that they would meet again the following weekend. He didn't remember the drive home; his mind was full of images of her grace and elegance. He couldn't help himself; as he imagined her naked in his bed, he felt a small wave of heat rise inside him.

THE DAYS TOOK their time in passing. He wanted to tell all of his friends about his new lover, but he thought they might think he was ridiculous to feel so much so soon. Why was he so hopeless when it came to playing it cool? Occasionally, he noticed an uncomfortable feeling, as if he was somehow doing something wrong and that he should be alone; that perhaps he should find himself a little more before getting involved with another woman. But he didn't like 'shoulds' and life had brought this gorgeous woman into his life for a second time, and now he was available. How could he possibly be expected to turn down such an unexpected and beautiful gift?

His articles and blogs took a back seat to his new literary outlet, and their connection grew as he wrote her long emails and they began to message each other more frequently. He tried his best not to text too often, partly because he didn't want her to know how much he longed for her as she might think him to be too needy. Then, once he had sent a message, his attention on other things was always compromised by awaiting her reply. Sometimes, while he did his best not to wait, he would find himself worrying that he might have said the wrong thing or offended her in some way. As a writer, he loved the power of the written word, but in writing to her, he became desperately aware of its limitations and how easy it could be to misinterpret the tone or cadence of what he had typed. He didn't want to do anything that might upset her. She was interested in him, that much was sure, but he always had this feeling that she could disappear at any moment and say that she didn't want to see him again. And, anyway, he didn't want to write to her; all he really wanted was to be with her.

The days blended together until at last, Saturday evening arrived, when they had arranged to meet. At her suggestion, they were to meet at another pub, but this time they would go on to an Indian restaurant nearby that she knew. Oddly, they arrived at the same time, and he hurriedly parked so that he could run over and open her car door. As she got out, her warm padded jacket was unzipped, and he could see that she wore a pretty red top that matched her black cotton skirt with seams of red and multicolored patterns. A simple cord held a smooth pewter pendant below her throat. Her alluring eyes narrowed and glinted, while an innocent smile spread across her face as if she knew what he was thinking. He beamed from ear to ear in semi-disbelief that she was even more beautiful than he remembered.

"Hello," she said.

"Hi," he replied.

He took her cool hand in the warmth of his. They decided not to go to the pub, and they walked the short distance down the lamp lit high street that took them directly to the restaurant. She said that she was hungry and when asked if he was hungry too, he said that he was. But the truth was that he didn't really know. He should have been ravenous since he had eaten little all day, but his stomach was so full of butterflies. Besides, a different sort of appetite was alight within him.

He hardly noticed the food or the other people. The polite visits from the waiter were an unwanted intrusion. They took it, in turn, to share a little more about each other, but again he preferred to listen as he could focus all of his attention on her. At times his concentration would waver, and her words would become vague sounds in the distance while his mind wandered. What he really wanted was for her to stand up in front of him and turn around slowly so that his eyes could drink in the curves, the rise and fall of her woman's body.

To him, women were the embodiment of the Goddess, the feminine essence of creation. There was something magical and mysterious about their powerful, captivating energy and awesome ability to grow and birth new life from the darkness of the womb.

He did his best to pay attention to what she was saying. His secret wish was briefly granted when she left for the bathroom, and this time he watched unashamedly as her swaying hips sauntered across the restaurant. By the time they had paid the bill, it was almost eleven o'clock, and the short walk meant that they arrived much too soon at the car park. Sensing that she too was disappointed that the evening was coming to an end, he asked her if she would like to sit a while in the car and continue their conversation. She replied, with a hint of shyness, that she would. As they sat in the semi-darkness of the car, he could contain himself no longer.

"May I kiss you?" he asked for the second time.

"You may."

He leaned over and for the first time felt the silken feel of her hair brush his hand as he held the back of her head and eased his lips upon hers. This time they were not cool, they were warm, and his lips lingered a little, while hers parted and yielded willingly to the gentle touch of the tip of his hot tongue. He pulled her closer, and their mouths and tongues met fully with a fierceness and passion that surprised him. The seemingly innocent and shy woman was gone, and they kissed long and slow while their arms held each other close and tight.

When the need for more air became too much to bear, he drew back and sat looking out of the windscreen while his chest rose and fell, and his breathing slowly began to settle.

He looked across at her in disbelief, amazed by her transformation. The innocent girl had been replaced by the wild, fiery Goddess, Lilith.

After he had caught his breath and the silence had stretched as far as it could he looked at her with a grin on his face.

"I am not too fond of this handbrake," he said.

She laughed. "Is that a subtle hint?" she asked. "Would you like to sit in the back seat?"

"I think it may be a bit more comfortable," he explained with a cheeky grin.

She looked around outside to see if anyone was about, but the car park was quiet.

"Okay," she said.

In the back of the car, it was much more comfortable! Pretty soon she was sat on his lap facing him with her legs on either side of his. They kissed like he had never kissed before, their wet lips parted, and their mouths opened wide to allow their agile tongues to dance together like two serpents coupling. It was as if their mouths were two halves of a whole that had finally been reunited. His hands were free to explore the contours of her back and neck and the most wonderful yielding flesh of her shapely hips. He untucked her blouse from her skirt and shivered at the feel of her warm, soft, silken skin and the delicate lace at the top of her cotton knickers. She clutched and clawed at his firm shoulders and ran her fingers through his long thick hair. In the back seat of a blue Peugeot in a semi-lit car park, heaven had arrived on earth. Nothing existed apart from their passion, their longing that circled and danced and spiraled around and through them. She sighed and moaned as his hands roughly, and then gently, worked their way exploring every inch of her neck, back, and hips. Her sensuous noises fueled his desire for her because he knew that she would be wet for him.

Almost two hours passed and finally, they rested as if they both knew that they could take things no further. Despite the heat of their aroused bodies, it was a cold February night. After holding each other in the dark stillness for a while, she shivered and, on looking at her watch, reported that it was nearly 2:00 am. He tucked her in as best as he could, and she removed herself as gracefully as possible from his lap. On leaving the car, they embraced tenderly under the sky in the chill night air. He saw her safely to her car, and she drove away into the night. While he waited for the condensation to clear from his windscreen, he whispered words of gratitude to the night while he felt the buzz of exhilaration and passion slowly ebb from his body. When he felt able to drive, he turned the ignition, shifted the gear lever, released the handbrake, with a grin on his face, and drove away.

CHAPTER 3

He carried on with the rest of his life as best he could. Often, he felt as though he was just killing time. Really, he was just waiting for when he would be with her again.

Sometimes, he would find himself rolling a cigarette outside his flat, on the little bench. While he smoked, he would lose himself in delicious imaginary realms in anticipation of the next time, they would be together. The scenes would be varied to some degree, but mostly he imagined them lying naked together in his bed. He would be propped up on his elbow, and his right hand would be lovingly exploring and caressing the silkiness of her warm naked flesh, while his eyes drank in her magnificent womanly form.

The motivation to keep up his daily writing commitments waned a little more as his passion for expression through the written word had found a new private audience. The book he was working on lost its rhythm and came to a halt. Without the flow, he needed to put an extraordinary effort into writing his blogs and articles that were part of his daily writers' life. Their texting became more frequent, although he was still a little cautious. He wasn't one for playing games, but he didn't want to appear too needy and scare her off. Sometimes he would wait a short while before responding to her so that she might not know that he had dived on his mobile as soon as he heard the sound of her incoming message. On other occasions when he had texted and heard nothing back for a while, he would reread his words, worrying that he might have upset or offended her by what he had written. He knew that she liked him, that much was obvious, but he didn't really know if she felt the same way as he did. He laughed out loud and chided himself when he remembered his initial plan to take things slowly!

Fortunately, she was usually quick to respond to his texts even though he knew she was always busy. Still, he would find himself feeling insecure. The messages were like scraps from the table, little morsels of connection. All he really wanted was to be with her, to be in her presence; she was the banquet. He just wanted to be with her all the time.

Early one Wednesday, as morning edged its way in and the night retreated, he lay awake under the snugness of his duvet, and suddenly an idea found him. He decided that he wanted to do something so that she would know how special she was to him. Rising swiftly from his bed he went to the living room where he chose an appropriate card from the drawer in his desk and wrote a few tender lines inside. The plan was to drive to her cafe, find her parked car and leave the card under the windscreen wiper.

But no sooner was the card tucked away in the sealed envelope than his mischievous mind began sowing seeds of doubt. He wasn't sure if it was such a good idea. What if she felt he was a bit over the top? What if she needed more time to settle into their togetherness? They had only known each other for a few weeks and met a couple of times. He put his coat on and dismissed his fearful thoughts as he grabbed his keys and left.

Her café was about forty minutes away. He arrived at his intended destination and drove around for a while, looking. What if he couldn't find her car?

He didn't want to surprise her by turning up unannounced at the café as she would be busy; a few moments with her would only leave him missing her more. He just wanted her to know how much he felt for her.

Then he saw her little green car parked by the side of the road in a line of other parked cars. He pulled over and crossed the road on foot, feeling suddenly rather self-conscious as passers-by might think that he was up to no good. Shrugging off his concern he lifted a windscreen wiper to place the envelope underneath. The message within was short and sweet.

"Darling, I am not sure if you know how beautiful you are. I think of you much too often, and I am counting down the time until we can be together on Saturday. With Love."

As he walked away, he took another glance inside the car to make sure that it was indeed hers and reassured at the sight of her coat on the back seat, he drove away.

That evening when she arrived home from work, she called him. It was clear that she was delighted, and she appreciatively thanked him for such a romantic gesture. He had never really thought of himself as romantic and, as far as he was aware, he had never been before. He couldn't avoid the fact that he was behaving very differently with this woman than he ever had done before. Was this love? If so, what had he experienced before? What was this woman doing to him? Why did he feel so strongly about her? Surely this couldn't just be lust!

They had agreed to go out for a meal again on the following weekend but, no matter how empty his stomach was, his appetite would inevitably vanish when he was with her. This evening was no exception, and he moved his chicken biryani around the plate, eating a little every so often. The next day he couldn't remember the details of their conversation, but he knew it had flowed easily and naturally. At times there were pauses, but they both seemed comfortable with the silence. Often, he would use these moments to unashamedly examine the features of her beautiful face more closely. The brightness of her blue, almond shaped eyes and their sparkle that intensified when she smiled; her charming nose, her delicate lips that held the promise of delights; the way her pale skin seemed to invite his caress. He wanted to drink in every detail of her. She offered little resistance to his attention, but at times she would smile shyly and look down. She knew what he was thinking, and he liked that she knew. He couldn't help but think again about the first time that they would lay together naked and then he would find himself adjusting his position on the chair awkwardly, suddenly self-conscious of the physical result of his arousal.

After the waiter had cleared away their plates, he looked bashfully across the table at her.

"I have a confession to make," he said.

She looked surprised and a little concerned, but she said nothing.

He explained that it was still early, and he wanted to spend some more time with her. The pubs were all closing, so there weren't many other options than to sit in the car, as she had already declined his offer to come back to his place. He had thought ahead and planned for this situation and stowed his duvet in the back seat of his car.

"I brought my duvet that you might be warmer in the car, in case you would like to drive somewhere quiet for a cuddle?"

She still looked a little shocked, but she laughed, too. She playfully admonished him and told him that he was outrageous. He took this as a compliment, agreed that he was, but that he only had her comfort and warmth in mind!

He watched her for a moment while she paused and took stock of the situation. She was weighing up the risk and deciding if she felt safe enough to park in a quiet place on a dark night with a man that she had only actually met a few times.

Soon, they were driving down a dark lane to a place that she knew. They arrived at a church where there was a small car park. From the back seat of the Peugeot, a few moments of conversation soon gave way to a more beautiful, primal form of communication; she straddled his lap as she had done before and their bodies and mouths were pulled together like a magnetic force that was powerful and strong.

Later, they sat side by side with the duvet around their shoulders, allowing the sensuous energy of their togetherness to settle. He suggested, not for the first time that they should meet at his place so that he could cook for her. The duvet had been a step in the right direction. She had been warmer, it was more comfortable, and they had stayed together for longer. However, he knew that he still wanted more, and he sensed that maybe she was also ready to open herself more fully to him. To his delight, she agreed to his suggestion, and it was agreed that they would meet at his flat the following weekend.

THE WEEK WAS extra challenging because he felt so ridiculously horny all the time. She had sent him a couple of selfies, and he would find himself gazing at these; his mouth would start watering, and his imagination would fast forward to all sorts of erotic scenarios that would happen on the coming Saturday night. He liked to imagine that she would arrive and he would immediately take her by the hand and lead her to the bedroom where he would lay on the bed, watching as she slowly removed her clothes as he had requested. He would ask her to slow down so that he could fully savour the moment, knowing that the most delicious lovemaking was about to begin. The anticipation of being naked with her for the first time was intense.

One time, his mind began to wander as he drove down the motorway on his way to an appointment. He felt his energy shift as little waves of warm excitement rippled through his torso and, at the thought of them together, he felt himself becoming hard. That evening, ignoring the feeling of vulnerability, he decided to text her about his interesting motorway experience. He was curious to see what her response would be and it was another opportunity to let her know how attractive he found her. She responded with firm words about driving safely and added a flirtatious comment. It was clear that she liked the fact that he was so turned on by her.

He felt like a little boy at Christmas, counting down the sleeps until Santa would visit and he was allowed to open his presents. After what seemed like an eternity, Saturday arrived. After his morning Tai Chi and a glass of fresh apple, celery and ginger juice, he drove up to the hills, parked the car and walked along the stony path to the ridge. He loved being with the hills. They were his best friend, his therapist and until he had met her, they had been his lover. Although he often took the same route, he loved the fact that no two walks were ever the same. The light, the temperature, the foliage on the trees, the sun, the moon, the birds, the ever-changing sky all guaranteed a unique experience. It didn't matter what the weather was doing; its variety was like the array of human emotions, and in his world, all feelings were to be welcomed or at least accepted to fully experience the sensuous miracle of being alive. During summer he took his top off and walked barefoot at times. In the winter, he wrapped up warm, jacket zipped, with his hat, gloves, and scarf for company. He loved the contrast of the winter bleakness and the gentle nurturing quality that pervaded the spring and summer months.

But on this day, he hardly noticed the beauty around him. His mind was full of a different type of beauty.

On returning home, he vacuumed the floors and cleaned the bathroom. He wanted the place to be at its best, and he felt as though he were preparing his humble home for a royal visit. He put some good cooking music on and began preparing the chicken and chorizo paella that he had promised her. He wasn't the best cook in the world, but he had half a dozen dishes that he liked to prepare. They were usually tasty enough. He had bought a good bottle of white wine which was happily cooling in the fridge. He felt very alive and enjoyed the waves of excitement that kept rising through him. When he thought about her, his face would break out into an enormous grin. His mind was driving him crazy with erotic images, and he had to keep reminding himself that it was by no means guaranteed that they would make love together tonight. He tried to convince himself that he didn't mind too much, as long as he was with her, but he did. He was so hungry for her.

He wanted the first time that they made love to be special, and so he prepared a little ceremony by way of marking the sacredness and beauty of their togetherness. He didn't know whether the night for the ceremony would be tonight, so the incense, feather, and candle sat innocently on top of the cabinet, just in case.

He regarded women with a mixture of amazement and inspiration. To him, they were unfathomably superior to men. He had been certain in his reverence from a young age. With respect, love, and honour for the right woman, sex could become a sacred act, a chance for a sacred union that was both mystical and divine.

He showered slowly, allowing the hot water to fall over his naked body. He wanted to be clear and clean of everything that had happened throughout the week. He washed his long brown hair and shaved the sides of his face being careful not to cut into his goaty beard.

Finally, he was ready for her. He busied himself around his flat choosing some simple tasks that required his attention but needed very little concentration, since his mind was all over the place with anticipation. Eventually, a message on his mobile phone announced that she was leaving her place and would be with him shortly.

After one last inspection of the flat to make sure that everything was just so, he lay down on the bed and closed his eyes. He remembered the wise words of Winnie-the-Pooh who had said that the best thing about having a full honey pot was the bit just before you started eating because then the full experience lay ahead of you. He hoped that for the first time he would lay naked with her in his bed. She was his honey pot, and yet he had only tasted a little from the lid of the opened pot. His appetite for her sweetness was almost too much for him to contain.

He tried in vain to settle himself and relax into meditation on the bed, but the excited energy in his body was relentless, and he had to get up and move around. Finally, while he pottered around the kitchen adding some final touches to the paella, he heard footsteps descending the steps that led to his basement flat. And then there she was, framed by the doorway, wearing a long brightly coloured evening dress. Round her neck was a fine silver chain with a pretty pendant that rested upon a generous piece of exposed naked chest below her throat. Her golden blonde hair was freshly groomed, and he smiled, flattered at the fact that she had brushed it in the car on her arrival so that she would look her best for him. It had worked, she looked amazing. What impressed him most, though, was the small black overnight bag that she held in her hand. He did his best to contain his joy, but she must have felt it as he held her close to him in a firm embrace, sliding his hands down to steal a quick squeeze of her gorgeous bum. He showed her quickly around his cosy little home and, trying not to draw any attention to the act, he took the small black bag and left it alone in the bedroom.

His fantasy of taking her straight to bed soon vanished as it became clear that she was a little nervous and needed time to arrive. And just because she was open to staying the night, he couldn't assume anything. He poured them both a glass of wine, and they sat on the sofa together. She told him about her week, and he shared a little of his. He found it hard to focus on anything because it all felt so surreal. Was he really alone in his home with the most beautiful woman in the world?

As the wine began to work its magic, she relaxed and slowed down so that there were more pauses between her sentences. They nibbled on some pieces of cheese, thin cut slices of chorizo and olives and, gradually, he too began to relax and settle a little. As they ate paella, she began telling him more about herself and some of the experiences that had shaped her. He didn't have a dining table, and they sat Japanese style on cushions around the pine coffee table with a solitary candle illuminating their faces. They already knew quite a lot about each other from their conversations, but now she was ready to go a little deeper. She began telling him a little about her childhood, and he recognized that she carried a father wound that was similar to his own mother wound. His heart opened as he listened, and his sexual desire was soon surpassed by a strong feeling of gentle warmth and a sense of protection towards her. She too had experienced many challenges in her life, and as she spoke quietly, her vulnerability was alluring. He felt a deeper connection to her than he had experienced before. He looked across the low table into her stunning eyes and for the first time he saw himself. What a beautiful clear reflection she was.

"I see you," he said kindly, in a brief pause of her storytelling. He was talking to her, but he was also talking to himself.

Her childhood had been far from ideal. The dysfunctional family environment had often been extremely challenging, especially because she was such a sensitive child. As a result, she had learned from an early age that people were not to be trusted.

When she had finished sharing this difficult part of her story a soft silence descended. It didn't happen often, but he was lost for words and all he could say was.

"I am sorry."

He shuffled round the table and pulled her close to him and held her tenderly. He didn't want her to have suffered, and at the same time, he had already seen this pain in her. He knew that life can sometimes seem so cruel. The intimacy of the moment was exquisite. A soft velvet blanket seemed to embrace them, and the tenderness and vulnerability of the moment was beautiful. Time disappeared, and they breathed together for a while.

When the energy had passed, he left her for a while with the silence of her thoughts and began clearing the table. Before long, his busyness created enough of a shift in energy for the mood to lighten. He chose a Nessi Gomez album, which seemed to fit the depth and sweetness of the moment and while it played in the background, they snuggled up close on the sofa. Pretty soon they were entwined with their hands exploring the contours of each other's bodies and his lips appreciatively exploring her exposed, naked throat. He found a special place at the nape of her neck which when kissed would cause her back to arch and soft moans of pleasure to ooze from her wide-open mouth. He loved the sounds of her bliss.

But the sofa was soon much too restrictive as the sexual energy ascended in wave after wave through his body. Pulling himself away from her he stood up and offered her his hand. She took it lightly and looked into his eyes with a look that said 'yes'.

He led her to the bedroom where they kissed again. He enjoyed it when she stood where his fingers could more easily explore the undulations of her body. It was not by chance that they stood in front of the full-length mirror where his eyes could enjoy the view of her from behind. For a moment they stood looking at each other in the soft, orange glow from the salt lamp. His body felt electrically charged, yet he took his time, knowing that this moment was so precious; it was not to be rushed.

He unzipped her dress, and it fell easily around her ankles revealing a wonderful view of her semi-nakedness in her matching underwear. He noted the gentle folds of her belly, the rise and fall of her goddess-like figure and it fired his longing for her. He took a step back and asked her to turn around slowly so that he could allow his eyes time to take in her beauty as she stood before him. She hesitated for a moment and then did as he asked.

When they were again face to face, she approached him and slowly undid the buttons down the front of his shirt and then slid it from his shoulders, her warm hands carefully stroked the firmness of his shoulders before running her hands over the hair on his chest. His body pulsed as he tried to slow his breathing and contain the surges of passionate energy that were rising within him.

Then, her delicate fingers undid his belt and the buttons on his jeans. He stepped out from his fallen trousers and asked her to turn around again. This time he stopped her carefully while her back was turned and fumbled clumsily at the strap of her white cotton and lace bra, causing her to giggle and him to curse under his breath. And then they were both almost naked. He knelt down and slowly slipped her matching knickers from around her womanly hips, over her thighs and allowed them to fall to the carpet. He stood, and she did the same with his black boxer shorts. They were both deliciously naked.

"Wait a moment," he said and disappeared back into the living room. He returned with the candle, the feather, and the sage incense.

"I would like us to hold a little ceremony to mark the sacredness of this moment with you. Would that be okay?"

A smile spread across her face, and she nodded.

He asked her to become fully aware of her breath, quieten her mind as best she could and to feel the magic of the moment. With the lighted candle, he lit the sage. He used the feather to waft the sweet smoke over her body from the crown of her golden blonde hair to the tips of her delicately painted toenails. He handed the feather and sage to her, and she did the same for him, smudging him from head to toe. Afterward, they sat back to back on the floor with a brightly coloured blanket wrapped around both of them so that it appeared as if there was one multi-coloured body with two heads. They sat, and he first said a little prayer out loud invoking The Great Mystery to bless and honour them. Then he prayed silently that he would be able to leave behind any old fears from past relationships and that he would always be committed to traveling deeper into the realms of the sacred masculine. He thanked The Great Mystery for bringing them together, brought his attention to his breath and allowed the excited energy in his body to settle a little.

After a little while of being sat, he could wait no longer. He rose from the blanket and held his hand out to her where she sat cross-legged looking up at him. She stood, and he carefully placed the candle on the bedside table. He threw back the duvet, and they climbed under the cool covers where they wrapped themselves around each other's naked bodies, and their mouths met with a new, as yet unexperienced passion and desire. His hands carefully explored every rise and fall of her silken curves while his tongue searched and explored every detail of her tender lips and mouth. He pulled her closer, wanting as much of her nakedness against him as possible. Then, gently but firmly, he took a hand full of her blonde hair and pulled her mouth away from his. He kissed her cheeks gently and then lingered at the special place at the nape of her neck causing her back to arch again and soft moans of pleasure to slip from her mouth. His mouth descended further and found a delicate, erect nipple which he kissed gently, caressing it with his tongue and then sucking a little. He moved his attention to the other breast, which also yielded willingly to his attention, while her fingers gripped his shoulders.

He whispered to her of her beauty and how hungry he was for her, and she responded with a deep sigh, and suddenly her body began to tremble; gently at first, but then more and more violently.

"Are you okay?" he asked, a little concerned.

"Yes," she replied. "I am not sure what's happening."

Based on her trembling, he guessed that she was experiencing kundalini energy. He knew a little about kundalini and that it involved the arising of energy that has been coiled at the base of the spine since birth. It is said to emerge as a result of an awakening of consciousness and furthers our connection with source energy, sometimes known as prana or chi.

Unusual bodily reactions are common, such as vibrations, jolts, and spasms, due to energy moving through the body.

The chemistry, the magic between them seemed to be so intense, so aligned that the energy had awoken something deep within her.

"We can stop if you like?" he offered.

"No way" she said. "Shut up and carry on!"

He laughed and, needing no further encouragement, continued his exploration of this yet uncharted and divine territory.

A hand found its way down over her soft belly to the warm, smooth flesh between the tops of her thighs and he paused, enjoying the moment of anticipation, knowing that she too knew where his fingers would soon be. He looked up at her before sliding his hand down to part her thighs, his fingers moving swiftly on to gauge her wetness; it was abundantly clear that she was ripe for entering. She was deliciously wet. His fingertips gently stroked and massaged her swollen petals as she gently moaned and sighed with pleasure at his loving and gentle touch.

His hungry mouth abandoned its pleasure at her breasts for a moment so that he could climb carefully on top of her. He parted her thighs a little more with his knees while he lowered himself down carefully until he almost rested upon her. Their eyes were locked together. Her face looked so different while she lay on her back; so innocent and vulnerable. Again, he noticed that otherworldly presence that she had about her.

He lowered himself a little more until he could feel the heat of her soft moistness on him and he held himself there for a moment while he looked deep into her eyes. Then he could contain himself no longer, and he allowed his arms to bend and his weight to fall a little so that he slid effortlessly inside her.

Her back arched again, and this time she let out a loud, full moan of pleasure, and he kept perfectly still for a moment, deep inside her, all the time watching her eyes dance and flicker in the subtle light. His hips came to life, and he pushed and raised himself with a calm rhythm while their mouths and tongues remained locked together in pulsing passion.

Her fingers and nails clawed at his back until he took both wrists in one hand and purposefully placed them above her head on the cream cotton pillow. The intensity of the moment rose even more as she lay under him, trusting and open. He found himself thrusting harder and deeper inside her, spurred on by the increase in volume and intensity of her gasps and moans of ecstasy. She looked, felt, sounded, tasted and smelt delicious as their hips danced their dance and her back arched and relaxed time after time.

Every now and then he would slow down and relax a little to catch his breath and allow himself to drink her in with his eyes. When he could no longer control himself, he let himself go, and primal energy poured forth, finding some release in a low growl that came from deep in his belly. He forced himself, every last millimeter, inside her and a stronger rhythm released droplets of sweat from his back and chest that leaked one by one onto her naked breasts and belly. Her panting increased as her hips began to contract and relax, faster and faster while heavenly sounds emanated from her mouth revealing that she was on the edge of orgasm. She screamed loudly without reserve, and he eased off a little sensing that the waves of pleasure coursing through her body were at the very edge of what she could handle. Eventually, the intensity seemed to subside and when she was almost recovered, he again raised himself up a little and kissed her tenderly on the mouth before thrusting again deep into her gorgeous, wet softness. The sensory feast of the woman that lay beneath him drew forth his last remnants of energy and he forced himself inside her over and over again until small waves of fire began to emanate from his loins, rising quickly in intensity until, with a primal cry and one last push, he let go deep inside her. She held him tightly to her while his heaving chest rose and fell.

Totally spent, he rested his saturated body on hers. After a while, his breathing began to find a gentler rhythm. Waves of energy rose up his spine and his back arched with a life of its own and tears filled his eyes. He kissed her repeatedly on her forehead and cheeks while her hands tenderly caressed his back. After a moment, he carefully slid himself from within her. As he moved from on top of her, he kissed her belly, and then they lay side by side in the silence holding hands. His mind was perfectly still as he savoured the beautiful feelings and sensations in his body.

After a while she turned and looked at him.

"No one has ever made love to me like that before," she said.

He smiled and stroked her hair, and in his head, he heard a voice say. 'And they never will.'

They lay together in the candlelight and talked softly about things that mattered to them and once again the shaking and vibrating would occasionally move her body. The movement seemed to correspond to when he was speaking about his beliefs about Life and Love and The Great Mystery. He asked if she was okay, to which she responded that she was and that she needed to talk about something. She seemed a little apprehensive as she began speaking about the unusual vibrations and energy that was happening in her body. She explained that it had happened a few times before, but that it was happening much more often since she had met him. He reassured her that it was not a problem for him and that she should do some research on kundalini energy. It was something he had heard of happening before and was sometimes associated with sacred lovemaking. Secretly, he felt that this occurrence was further evidence that there was something special and important in their coming together.

Before long, as they talked and he caressed the silkiness of her skin with his finger-tips, he felt the rising wave of desire within him and knowing that she too was ready, they made love again.

His hunger satiated, they lay together with her head resting on his chest and his arm around her shoulder while they again listened to the silence. Then she kissed him gently on the cheek and breathed a whispered 'goodnight' before turning over and pulling the duvet up under her chin.

"Good night my darling," he said.

IN THE MORNING they made love again. She shared his appetite for morning sex, and he was delighted that this gorgeous creature seemed to have a sexual appetite that was equal to his own.

They showered and dressed and ate a leisurely, late brunch together before heading out under the sky to walk on the hills that he loved so much. As they sauntered along hand in hand, their conversation ebbed and flowed, and they laughed and stopped to hold each other and kiss unashamedly in full view of the passing clouds and the big sky.

But time was cruel and before long the day was done. They laid together once again, in the warm sanctuary of his bed, their breath gradually settling from the exertion of their lovemaking.

Sleep took them swiftly and all too soon the morning had arrived when it was time for her to leave. He felt a sinking feeling in his stomach as she packed her bag. One last kiss and embrace, and she was gone.

"Back to reality," he said as he opened his diary to remind himself of his commitments for the day.

CHAPTER 4

Being a self-employed author had its advantages. There were meetings, interviews, and events around the country to attend, but to a large extent, he was in control of his own diary. He was comfortable writing for different audiences and, though the majority of his work was for adults, his most recent accomplishment was a children's book. He loved the idea that little children all around the world would be going to sleep after being read his story by a loving parent. As they drifted off, he hoped that the positive messages woven into the story would permeate deep into their unconscious and their dream world. The book he was supposed to be working on was about the awakening of the sacred masculine as it was something that he inherently felt part of. It was as if his whole life journey had been a training exercise to awaken his divinity and the realisation that he had a part to play in healing the discord between the masculine and feminine. But for now, it was on hold. The words would not flow, and he recognised that the experiences with this captivating woman would probably inform the content of the book. In these situations, there needed to be time for the integration of his experiences before he could discern how they could best compliment the message that he wanted to convey through his writing. So, for the most part, he focused on smaller tasks and aspects of his work as a writer.

But, for her, life had more structure. She worked hard in the café from Tuesday to Saturday and often studied or met up with her friends in the evenings. She loved her café and often shared heart-warming stories of conversations and encounters that took place there. Her loving and caring energy meant that it was much more than people's hunger for food that was met by visiting the café. Her customers always left feeling cared for, heard and seen.

He had found his way of making the world more beautiful, and so had she.

Sundays and Mondays were her days off from her café and, to his delight, she opted to spend most of this time with him. Before long they had settled into a rhythm, he stopped booking weekend engagements and whenever possible kept his Mondays free. She would usually arrive at his place on a Saturday evening, tired from her week's work, but he was pleased to see her however tired she was. So far he had not visited her home; she assured him that this was because his flat was set in such idyllic surroundings which meant that they could enjoy their wonderful walks under the sky. He was in no rush to see her place as he loved playing host and taking care of her when she arrived as his cherished guest at his flat. He had always been a little more comfortable at giving than receiving. But in the back of his mind, he wondered if she hadn't invited him to her place because she didn't trust him.

He always cleaned his home meticulously in preparation for her visits. And he would shower with focused intention so that he could be free of any old past energy and be fully new and clean and present for her arrival. Candles would be lit, and incense burned to ensure that the space was thoroughly cleared for their special time together.

There was always something good to eat when she arrived, although she often insisted on bringing a contribution that she had made herself or, occasionally, tasty left-overs from the café.

The countryside where he lived was alive and rich with natural beauty. For him, the earth was his church, his place of prayer. For her, it was the wind that she loved most. They were both lovers of nature, and this meant that whenever they met at his place their walks would often be up on the hills where she would delight in the wind and his bare feet would kiss the earth. As the warm weather arrived, picnics became a regular occurrence; when the weather turned chilly, they would stay huddled together under the warmth of the picnic blanket.

The times between their heavenly weekends together became a little easier for him but, like an unquenchable thirst, he always felt as though he wanted more of her. By Thursday he could hardly remember what she felt like and he needed to hear her voice, to breathe her in and feel her skin against his. He often wanted to phone, but he was frightened that she would find him too intrusive, so he rarely called. She always seemed to be so busy. It was difficult to balance his desire to connect with her. He never wanted to appear too needy, but he also wanted to make it clear that she was important to him, that he wanted to connect with her as much as possible. To add to things, his fear of rejection was sometimes triggered when she didn't return his call when he left a phone message for her. What could have been simple and easy became challenging for him, so he rarely phoned.

He appeased his lack of courage when it came to phoning her with the knowledge that she was actually more comfortable with messaging; in the evenings she would be tired from her long days' work, and all the socialising with customers left her wanting her own company, peace, and quiet. Still, the perceived long gaps between spoken communication kept him wondering if she was hiding something from him. In his mind, it seemed as though he was much fonder of her than she was of him. Was there something he was not seeing? He knew that he was a little bit bowled over by her and was once again amused at his early thoughts of taking things steadily.

It often felt as if she was just out of reach, like she was a slippery golden fish that might fall from his grasp at any moment. Somehow, he could find no security in their relationship when she was not with him, but slowly he began to get more accustomed to being with these uncomfortable feelings. The truth was that there were usually only five days between their times together. He could manage that.

CHAPTER 5

April saw the arrival of his birthday. They decided that if the weather allowed, they would do what they both loved and go for a picnic. His special day fell on a Monday, so she arrived midday on Sunday with the intention of leaving early on Tuesday morning so that they could spend the whole of his birthday together. He couldn't have asked for a better birthday present.

Tupperware containers, which she brought with her, were placed in the fridge and there was a picnic basket with strict instructions for him not to look inside. He wasn't so interested in what they would eat, he was just glad that he would get to share his special day with her. What a marvelous gift she was!

That evening as they sat hand in hand on the sofa in the candlelight, she turned to him. "I have something that I need to tell you."

His heart missed a beat, though once he had scanned her face and looked into her eyes, he relaxed a little.

She told him that she had had some unusual energetic experiences over the last few years and that the variety and intensity of the experiences appeared to have increased since they had met. From her description of what had happened, it was clear that she was psychic and clairvoyant to some extent. Sometimes, she told him, she would find herself in an altered state. She would have visions or hear voices that were very clear and very different from the normal experience of how thoughts happen in the mind. He was no stranger to the unusual; in his rich and unconventional life, he had accumulated a collection of experiences that were impossible to explain with his rational mind. He knew that beyond the limitations of the small pond of the mind and what his senses could perceive, there was an unexplored ocean that he had only ever really dipped his toe into.

Relief flooded through him as she spoke, and he wondered whether what she began to share had something to do with the incredibly powerful hold that she seemed to have over him. Why were these energetic experiences happening more since she had met him? He had never experienced anything quite like this intensity of energy before; he had to admit that he was completely under her spell. Perhaps this explained the otherworldly feeling he got from her. He breathed a sigh of relief that his intuition had not been totally misguided, that there really was some deep purpose and meaning to their meeting. It was as if this information she was now sharing confirmed that his attraction to her was not just superficial; it was not only her physical beauty, but also about a deep soul attraction or contract.

Their initial meeting at the author fair and then finding each other again nine months later when they were both single had seemed beyond coincidence. He had never really believed in 'the one,' a soul mate that we would meet in our lifetime and then share the rest of our days with. And yet, secretly, he hoped that this might be the case because it meant that he would never have to lose her.

It appeared that they had been destined to meet again. He hoped that he was about to get a clearer understanding of what on earth was going on. Fear and excitement arose in him at the same time; he breathed a few times deeply, brought his awareness to his heart and settled his mind as she continued to talk.

She spoke in a way that was different than ever before and, as she did so, her words would sometimes be interrupted momentarily by little convulsions and tremors that shook her. She apologetically explained, once again, that this was one of the things that was happening more often since they had met. He reassured her that it was really nothing to worry about, that it was probably just kundalini energy moving, which could trigger months or years of new sensations. It wasn't a problem for him.

As he listened, she seemed to become more at ease. She began to speak of an experience a few days earlier while she sat quietly in meditation. She had asked for guidance as to what was happening to her. She increasingly felt that something big was taking place for her, as if she was no longer the person she used to be, but, was unsure of who she was becoming. Her guidance arrived with a clear response. A voice, as she described, that was also not a voice, arose in her mind. It said, simply 'Bring him home.'

She said this had made no sense to her. 'But what does that mean?' she asked 'them.'

But she just heard the same words repeated 'Bring him home.'

She looked at him questioningly. "I don't know what it means, but I knew they were talking about you."

Something strange stirred deep within him. A wave of hot and cold energy surged through him, and he turned away as tears began to fall from his eyes. They were tears of sadness and relief and joy all at the same time; they were new tears. He knew very clearly what the words meant. For the last twenty years, he had been on a rollercoaster journey of healing and transformation. He had always had a sense of living in the world, but not really being of it. He increasingly felt as if he were a stranger in a foreign land and he knew that the way home to peace and love was through the doorway of his heart. But he didn't really know how to access and transform all the fear and shadowy emotions that seemed to block his full ability to feel joy and peace. There was a sense that the journey was reaching a critical place, that he was on the cusp of arriving at a deeper, more peaceful place within himself. But, like an elusive shadow, it always seemed just out of reach. In that moment he knew that this was why they had come together. They both carried missing pieces of the jigsaw that they were to share to find their way back to the truth of love and life and heal their wounded hearts.

She held him tenderly while his tears fell, and her body trembled and shook. He hoped that this would mean that he could finally find ease in their togetherness now that he knew there was a divine purpose behind their meeting. As they held each other the words 'Bring him home' echoed inside him. For him, it was clear that this was the Goddess speaking to her.

Still, it was all rather vague. Could it mean that she would take him home to the doorway and then leave him? Was she coming all the way home too? Did this mean that they would come home and be together always? He felt a pang of terror inside and knew in an instant that, along with his desire to be with her was also an acute fear of not being with himself; of not being alone. He knew that he would have to let go of this irrational fear, especially since he knew that everything is interconnected, that aloneness is a trick of the mind and that we are all parts of a bigger whole in which we can never really be alone.

He was already aware that the fire of love is sometimes fierce and ruthless in its burning away of the false through conscious relationships. He knew in that moment that the journey home with her would not all be easy; that the road ahead would likely test his commitment to returning fully to his heart, and to love.

He kept all these thoughts to himself while she held him and after a little while the tears stopped falling. He tried to share some of his thoughts with her, but her expression led him to believe that she didn't really seem to understand what he was saying. He stopped talking and kissed her slowly and tenderly, from a place of awe and gratitude for the blessing of her and the mystery of life.

The atmosphere was soft and gentle. When he felt a little less tender, he asked if she would like a bath. Whenever she came to stay, he wanted to make the experience as lovely as possible for her. Partly because he loved looking after her, but partly because he wanted to make it all so precious that she would always come back. He liked to buy her favourite chocolate, biscuits, and wine. Sometimes, there would be other small gifts waiting for her, too.

But in truth, his motives regarding the bath were mixed! Yes, he wanted her to relax and nurture herself, but he also wanted to wash her; to soap all her gorgeous, naked body gently and lovingly. This was as much for his own pleasure as hers.

Part of the beautiful dance of connection is that as we give, we also receive. And when we receive gratefully, the giver receives so much, too. Love can be made visible in this way. 'Love' is a short, simple word, yet so much is contained within these four letters. In many ways, it had always been a mystery to him. He had always questioned himself when he had been with previous lovers. Is this love? But something was happening inside him, in his core, and he could only guess that this was something to do with love. If it was love, it was deeper than he had ever known before. He wanted to speak to her about it, but he was frightened that his words would be too clumsy, and his fear of vulnerability held him back. What if he told her that he loved her, and she didn't feel the same? How would he handle that with his fears of rejection?

Instead, he made a strong commitment to show her in every way possible how he felt about her and so he ran the bath. Actions speak louder than words, he reminded himself!

He watched her undress. He always loved seeing her nakedness revealed. It wasn't as if she had a glossy magazine model's body, but to him, it was divine because it was her. Sometimes she would casually mention her boyish hips or of how in some ways the aging process was difficult for a woman as society is so obsessed with youthful beauty. He could see that in places her skin was not as firm and smooth as it once might have been, but it didn't detract from her beauty. She was a middle-aged woman, and her essence was enhanced by the storms that she had endured and the light of her soul. Though it radiated mostly from her clear blue eyes, this essence embraced all of her like a soft, glowing mantle.

He lit some candles, put on some gentle music and added some lavender oil to the bath. He would have added some bubbles, but he didn't have any. He admonished himself briefly for the oversight before finding consolation in knowing that he had a new bar of natural coconut milk soap. Then he left her for a while in the sanctuary of the hot water and busied himself around the flat, preparing food and washing up in the kitchen.

After a short while, she called his name and invited him into the bathroom. He knelt beside the bath with the soap in his hands. They spoke a little in whispers as if they were at church, in a holy place. Focusing on his task, he first washed her slender neck. Then, taking each hand and lifting her arms one at a time, he allowed the soap to glide up and down her arms. At his request, she leaned forward so he could attend to her back, noting each birthmark and mole, careful to cover every single bit of pale skin. Then, her beautiful small breasts met the loving touch of his hands; he moved next to the tenderness of her belly and then, sliding his hands under her ankles, he lifted her legs one at a time so that he could caress every inch. His fingers brushed the extra softness between her thighs and waves of arousal permeated his body as he knelt beside her.

When he had washed all of her and could prolong the experience no longer, he leaned over so that he could kiss her long and full on her steamy, wet mouth. Then, he left her amidst the warm scent of coconut soap, lavender, and the mellow light.

She emerged in her white fluffy bathrobe with her blonde tresses tucked into an untidy bun on her head. He glanced at her from where he lay on the sofa and wondered how she always managed to look so divine. It didn't matter whether she had just finished applying her make up in preparation for going out in the evening or if she had just woken in the morning with tangled hair and sleepy eyes. There were many facets to her beauty, and he adored them all.

They ate a simple meal around the low table by candlelight and talked about the other strange experiences that were part of their personal journeys; how each individual adventure had in some way led them to the next, like stepping stones in the mist. Every now and again he would sigh with relief and joy as he remembered that he still had her all to himself for a whole day and two nights.

As if that was not wonderful enough, he also knew that soon they would again be naked together in his bed.

The following morning was his birthday. He waited under the warmth of the duvet while she busied herself around his flat. He liked it that she seemed at ease in his home. She returned to the bedroom with a tray of tea and cards and parcels. He opened the few cards that had arrived in the post and then she brought a cake she had made, with lighted candles shimmering. After a chorus of Happy Birthday, he blew out the candles, and she presented him with her card and gifts. Even her handwriting was beautiful, and her message was warm, loving and poetic. He unwrapped her gifts. There was a stunning and delicately ornate Moroccan candle lamp and a leather-bound notebook in which she had written inside 'To fill with your beautiful words.'

She always encouraged him to write and told him that he had the soul of a poet.

Of course, the only way that he could express his gratitude for her Birthday gifts was by making love to her! He pulled her onto the bed, and she offered little resistance as they kissed slowly and tenderly. His hands travelled their favourite journey around her naked contours, and her utterings of delight grew as his fingers found their way between her thighs. He knew what she liked best, and his only desire was to pleasure her in gratitude for all that she was and for her careful attention in making his Birthday a special day.

Eventually, when they both had their fill, they showered and dressed.

The weather, although a little chilly, was dry, and so after a leisurely breakfast, they began preparing for their picnic. He had already decided where they would go. It was one of his favourite places and was very different from his usual haunts on the open expanse of the hills.

They drove for twenty minutes as the main roads gave way to narrower and narrower lanes. The countryside here felt softer and more nurturing, and after crossing a couple of fields on foot, they arrived at the ancient oak tree that was their destination and chosen picnic spot.

He had never taken her here before. It was a very sacred place for him. There was something very magical and mysterious about the old oak. Many previous visitors had left ribbons tied to the low hanging branches, and small offerings littered the roots and folds of the gnarled bark.

It felt a bit as if he were introducing his beloved to his father for the first time to receive a blessing. As she approached the trunk of the majestic old tree, she stopped suddenly. With her arms outstretched and palms open, she moved forward again and placed them upon its trunk.

His eyes and heart wide open, he watched this unusual woman in front of him, who had come to grace him with her presence on his birthday. The birds sang in the nearby hawthorn hedge, and the white and grey clouds unhurriedly moved across the enormous, pale blue sky.

After spending a while with the tree, she turned and came into his arms. She told of how she could feel a deep sadness and kindness from the tree. At first, it was not sure about welcoming her; she had paused, but then it had given her permission to lay her hands upon it. Indeed, the oak was very old, all but a few of the boughs were dead. The life seemed to be ebbing slowly from it, though there was still a profound grace and majesty about its letting go of life. He wondered if the kindness and sadness she felt were her own or the oak's, but it didn't really matter. What mattered was that she was with him now, on the day that, forty-nine years earlier, had marked the beginning of the great adventure through the beauty and pain of his human experience. And he was so glad for all of it and so grateful to be alive. He thanked his mother silently for giving birth to him and felt a pang of sadness that she had left her body so soon after his birth.

They chose a reasonably flat spot to lay the picnic blanket and began to empty the contents of the basket. She had gone to great lengths to bake savoury pastries, as well as the cake, and had also packed his favourite Spanish tapas. The red wine was a little cooler than it should have been due to the weather, but there was little that could have spoilt the pleasure of their time together as they sat beneath the outstretched branches of the wise old oak. Wrapped in their coats they laughed and talked, eating and drinking in every moment of their time together.

When they had eaten enough, they packed up their picnic and huddled under the cosiness of the picnic blanket. The wind had lifted a little and the temperature began to fall. The weather seemed unable to dampen their spirits and to keep warm they took it in turns to run around the field cloaked in the blanket whooping and whirling with abandoned frivolity, while the other laughed at the ridiculousness of the spectacle.

Before they left the company of the beautiful, old oak, they stood embraced in each other's arms with the blanket wrapped around them. Her soft cheek was cold against his, and the warmth of the blanket enveloped them in their togetherness for a few moments; the rest of the world was but a distant memory. He knew that it was a birthday that he would always remember.

On arriving back to the comfort of his flat, she read her book while he made a few phone calls. She loved her books. They transported her to magical realms and far-away places of learning and adventure and had been a great comfort and escape for her when things had been difficult growing up. She spoke about her books as if they were her children and he loved it that they both shared a passion for the written word; he for writing and her for reading.

The evening drifted by too quickly. Occasionally, he would remember that she would leave him again the following morning and he would experience the familiar sinking feeling in his stomach. But he would dismiss the troublesome thought quickly and return to the moment with her.

They talked a lot about things that were personal to them. He loved listening to the gentleness of her feminine voice, it made it easier to give her his full attention. She told him that she was sharing secrets with him that she had never told anyone before; he was humbled and moved by her trust.

But, as the weeks of knowing her began to drift into months, he found himself wanting to speak of their future together. He was painfully aware that when she spoke about the future, it never seemed to include him. He didn't know if he was jumping the gun, but he so wanted her to be part of his future.

He had no real clear plans for the rest of his life, apart from finding peace within himself and doing what he could through his writing or by other means to make the world a more beautiful place. There was space for her in his future no matter what it might be, but he was unsure whether she felt the same about him. When he brought this up with her, she would dismiss his concern carelessly and assure him that of course, he was part of her future.

THEY WERE BACK in his favourite place: bed. Sometimes he was so full of desire that he wanted to enter her quickly, but he always made sure that he took his time. Making love too quickly was like gulping down a fine glass of wine. And anyway, he was happy to move at her pace. After all, he wanted to please her, as her pleasure was his pleasure. Soon, her golden hair was strewn untidily around her head on the pillow like a glowing aura; her smiling eyes looked up at him with a hint of shyness. She appeared heavenly. He gazed into her eyes lovingly until the pull was too great and his head descended slowly until his lips were upon hers and the dance of ecstasy began.

Arms, hands, legs all coiled and writhed like twisting, dancing tree roots, magically brought to life, as they explored the delicious nakedness of each other's hot bodies. Her mouth tasted so sweet, and her temporary shyness soon gave way to an intense passion. She demanded that he lie on his back while she mounted him. He loved being able to see all of her sat astride him as he lay on his back. His outstretched hands fondled the yielding softness of her beautiful breasts as he felt himself inside her sensual, warm wetness. Her moans of pleasure were music to his ears. Head thrown back, her face contorted in grimaces of pleasure while her hair, untidy and wild, framed her now flushed, red face.

When she was ready, she lay down on top of him and grinded and pulled herself over, with, in him. Her hands clutched his shoulders while his hands found their pleasure holding her ample buttocks in a vice-like grip. When she was done with him, when her cries had ceased, and he knew the waves of bliss had reduced a little, he rolled her over and entered her again with an all-consuming fierceness, pushing deep, deep inside her. He didn't feel the urge for release this time, and after a while, his body gently brought itself to rest silently on top of her. Their breaths fell in sync as he felt the thud of his heartbeat gradually relax. For a while, he lay with his head on her chest so that he could listen to her heart. Then, he raised himself up a little, and they just looked into each other's eyes.

He had never made love to a woman in this way before. When they were ready, they lay in the soft light together, side by side, while his breathing settled. With their fingers entwined they enjoyed the beauty of the energy that engulfed them both and filled the whole room. Every now and then he whispered some words to her that would arise from somewhere beyond him and the kundalini energy would invariably move her body to tremble a little. In this altered state, bliss was real and present.

Once the sweet energy had dissipated, they made the customary trip to the bathroom, and they were soon settled again under the covers in preparation for sleep to take them. Before rolling onto her side, she whispered "Goodnight."

"Goodnight darling," he said. "Thank you for a wonderful birthday."

He leaned over and kissed her one more time on the lips, and she rolled over, turning her back on him. He lay in the darkness and listened to her breathing change until he guessed she was asleep and then rolled over onto his side, tucked the duvet under his chin and drifted off.

He woke up to a text message from his neighbour who lived in the flat above. It seemed that their passion had been a little noisy for him and the message was a request to be a little more considerate. She laughed out loud when he told her, but he was a little annoyed. He loved the wild, noisy abandon of their lovemaking.

"If you can't relax when you are making love in your own home, when can you?" he protested.

She told him to try and not let it bother him. She was more concerned about the prospect of seeing him on the driveway, anyway.

"How am I ever going to be able to look him in the eye?" she asked with a giggle.

Her light-hearted words had an immediate calming effect on him.

"Let's not worry about it now," he said. "It's early, and he is bound to still be asleep. I seem to remember someone saying how she loved morning sex."

He looked at her with narrowed eyes in a mock menacing look and pulled her towards him and kissed her roughly. She didn't protest, and they made love, loudly and unrestrained!

CHAPTER 6

It was hard to say when things really began to change, but he noticed a marked and uncomfortable growth of unease in his mind. The first time that he really became aware of it was when she went away to Croatia for a long weekend with her son. In his mind, he was very happy that she was going away on an adventure with someone who meant so much to her, even though he would miss out on their weekend time together. But from his body there arose a fear which made him feel so insecure. As the days crawled by, he was shocked by the intensity of what he felt. He wanted to be open and honest with her about what was happening for him because he knew that she would sense his emotions from the short text messages that they exchanged. He also felt he could not call her and interrupt the lovely time that she would be having with her son because he was concerned that she would be turned off by his apparent insecurity.

He repeated over and over to himself that she would just be gone for a little while; soon, she would be back in his arms. It just didn't make any sense that he should feel such extreme emotions and longing and he found it difficult not to berate himself for being weak and pathetic.

He decided that he would be open and vulnerable and speak to her about his experience while she had been away. He wanted to be able to share everything with her; at the same time, he knew that she needed a strong man to walk beside her and his neediness was probably quite unattractive. If she was emotionally triggered by his sharing, then she might close down a little and withdraw. He knew he would feel this acutely and might cause him to become even more needy. He felt as if he were caught between a rock and a hard place. He changed his mind and decided that he would have to just feel and release his feelings by himself as best he could.

As the frequency and intensity of his emotional state ebbed and flowed, he fought a battle inside himself which he felt he was not winning. He realised that she was bringing to the surface old unresolved trauma from deep within that was related to the death of his mother as a child. He so wanted this not to be happening, but it was. It seemed as if there was nothing that he could do. He was at the mercy of something bigger and more powerful than he had faced before and the realisation that it might force a wedge between them terrified him.

By the time she had returned from Croatia, he had smoked much too many cigarettes, and his nerves were a little ragged. But as soon as she was in his arms again, everything felt better. His unease settled while she sat beside him on the sofa, sharing some of the experiences she had enjoyed most while she had been away. He was delighted that although she had returned a little weary from her busy time away, she had enjoyed her holiday. But there was also a part of him that felt some jealousy towards her son. He was uncomfortable with the thought but, could not deny that he wanted her to only have wonderful times with him.

As if she could read his thoughts, she asked him if everything was okay. It became increasingly apparent that she could feel when something was not quite right, which in truth, probably wasn't difficult; he always wore his heart on his sleeve. He shared a little bit of what he had been feeling while she had been away, by way of testing the water and seeing how she responded. She told him that she had known that all was not well for him while she had been in Croatia, but that she had done her best to reassure him. He suspected that she was not voicing all that she felt, and he thought he sensed a weary disappointment in him, but his perception was possibly being clouded by his emotions. She said that she was tired, and this meant that the conversation was over. He felt her withdraw and close a little. He didn't really feel that it had brought resolution, as if she had not really heard him, but at least he had shared some of what he felt. He believed that open, vulnerable and honest conversation was a powerful way of creating closeness and intimacy with another, but this was new territory for her. She didn't seem to fully understand, and he couldn't expect her to, as she had only ever been with men who were closed and uncommunicative. He knew that it was important that the energy between them was as clear as possible, which meant truthfully sharing any issues, fears or concerns that might arise while taking full responsibility and not blaming the other. Although he wanted to be able to share all of himself with this woman, he realised that this might not be the case; her willingness to remain in emotionally uncomfortable places seemed to be less robust than his. He would have to learn to find other ways of resolving the angst within him. Perhaps he just wanted to talk too much.

Fortunately, she had missed his physical presence while she had been away as much as he had missed hers. She spoke of missing the strength and passion of his body, and before too long they were naked together once again. When they made love that evening, he gave everything of himself and, although it arose from a loving place, he knew that it was also laced with fear of losing her. He postponed his release for as long as possible so that he might continue to pleasure her. He wanted to be the best lover that she had ever had so that any other challenges might arise between them the passion and merging of their lovemaking would ensure an unbreakable bond. How ironic that love and fear could so easily become bedfellows.

The next day the weather was kind to them, and he took her to a place she had not been before on the hills. They walked and talked, occasionally stopping to take in the magnificence of the view, or to lie down in the warm grass to kiss and caress each other. The warmth of the sun and the exertion of the route invited him to take his shirt off so that the sun could caress him, along with a gentle breeze that at times drifted by, too. He loved the feeling of the sun and wind on his naked body, and he knew that she admired his physical attributes. As they walked hand in hand, his fears and the pain of missing her while she had been away dissolved and seemed like a bad dream.

That evening, at his suggestion, they made plans and booked a mini break away together at a cottage in Devon by the sea. The idea that for the first time, he would have four whole days with her was wonderful. He wanted to show her how much he cared for her; arranging a romantic break together seemed perfect.

Before bed, they sat and watched a video on YouTube that he had happened to notice earlier in the week. It was all about 'twin flames' and 'soul mates.' He thought there may be some answers to his questions about the strength of his attraction, as he had heard about people meeting and experiencing a sense of two souls finally finding each other again. But, to his dismay, the video explained how twin flame relationships were often extremely tumultuous and not always destined to be long-term. Such relationships were often catalytic in nature and served as a fast track process for healing unresolved wounds and trauma. Only those most committed to deep spiritual growth would stay the course.

Soul mates, on the other hand, were described as more likely to make a lifetime partner. Try as he may, he couldn't help but see that their connection seemed to be a twin flame connection. He felt a familiar pang of anxiety at the idea that they might not always be together. He pushed the thought out of his mind and squeezed her hand a little tighter, grateful that the video was coming to an end.

As always, the morning came too soon, and she was gone again, but not before they had decided that the following weekend, they would meet at her cottage for the first time. He was keen to see her home, and he assumed that the fact that he was invited meant that she was beginning to trust him.

IN HER ABSENCE, the first couple of days passed relatively easily with the usual exchange of messages and memes by mobile phone. He hoped that his missing her would not grow too acute again. She would write in her messages that she missed him, but for some reason, he didn't really believe her. His mind only wanted to accumulate evidence that she would never really be 'his woman.' He convinced himself that the way she missed him seemed to be so light and easy compared to the uncomfortable longing that kept visiting him. Perhaps she was feeling the same as him, and he was just weak and not as adept at feeling the emotions as she was.

He studied the emoticons at the end of her messages too much. He noticed that she never sent any hearts; sometimes he even found himself counting the kisses she had sent. His mischievous mind kept searching for evidence that she was not falling in love with him so that he might keep his own heart safe and protected and not fully open. He chided himself for his ridiculous behaviour; he needed to get a grip. He repeated over and over in his head that everything was fine. But a new thought began to emerge that niggled at him. What if the insecurity he was feeling was not entirely the figment of his own imagination? What if there was something, she was not telling him? What if the image of the slippery fish was real and not just the product of his insecurity? If she were not being fully open and honest with him, it would explain why he felt a subtle lack of commitment from her, and maybe this was fueling his fears.

On the other hand, they had not known each other for that long, and it seemed reasonable that she would be cautious in opening fully and trusting him. She seemed to say all the right things, but perhaps it was more about what she was not saying that gave him such a sense of unease. He wanted to ask her so many questions, but he feared that she would find his probing too much. As a result, she might emotionally withdraw, which prevented him from speaking his truth fully.

In his mind he had already chosen her and, having learned from previous relationships, his commitment to her was unwavering. He knew that in the past things had come to an end partly because of his own unresolved childhood wounds. Previously, when things had got difficult, he would resort to an old coping strategy of smoking cannabis. It would help to take the edge off the uncomfortable emotions he was feeling and distract his mind, but he had pledged to himself that he would not use this avoidance strategy again. He was sick and tired of every relationship ending because of some old stories that were just ghosts from the past. He could no longer keep running from his distraught inner child. He had decided that whatever arose in this relationship, he would stand and face it. It was time to slay this dragon once and for all.

And so, as he had suspected, their connection was doing its work and bringing his fears and old, unfelt emotions to the surface, which to a large extent had nothing to do with what was happening in the present. He was just a little surprised at their intensity and how quickly the purging had begun. The honeymoon period appeared to be over. In fact, it had hardly existed at all, and the mysterious dance of love was doing its thing and clearing him out. He thought that much of his fear around intimate relationship had been transformed. However, this beautiful woman, who he was falling deeply in love with, was obviously touching places in him where there was more healing to be done. This time, he had metaphorically stuck his warrior's sword in the ground and had made a pledge to himself. Even though he feared being abandoned, his wish to be with this woman meant that he would stand and face whatever arose so that they could journey together into the magic of divine union.

HE DECIDED TO initiate some regular sessions with his mentor so that he could share some of the fears and feelings that were arising in him, be heard and receive clarity on what was happening. With the first meeting in the diary, he felt some relief, and during the week he busied himself with his work commitments. Still, not too much creative energy was being channeled into his work. Emails and letters became a regular way in which he expressed his feelings for her. On one of his trips abroad to Thailand, he had bought a stamp and some wax. He would always seal his handwritten letters and cards with the triple spiral design stamped into the melted wax. She loved receiving envelopes in the post and told him of how much she appreciated the thoughtfulness and care of these gestures.

The days merged into each other and his longing to be with her tainted his enthusiasm for other aspects of his life. He had a good community of friends, but his connection with them dwindled a little, perhaps because he felt that he didn't want to bore them with details about his relationship. He felt he had little else of value to talk about.

His frequent walks on the hills brought some solace as he greatly valued the growing intimacy that he felt with the natural world. Increasingly, as he wandered over hills and along paths, he would feel the presence of nature all around him. The beauty and serenity of the natural world were staggering. It was as if he was seeing with new eyes. But, even here, he would occasionally notice couples walking together, which would remind him that he wanted to be with her. Other times he would pass solitary figures that would also accentuate his aloneness and missing her.

CHAPTER 7

Sunday arrived, and he drove over to stay at her place as they had agreed. He felt excited that they would be together in her home for the first time. It was her turn to be the hostess, and he was pleased that she trusted him enough to allow him into her home.

As he walked up the path, she stood framed in the light beech doorway, looking as gorgeous as ever. He marveled at how lucky he was to have her in his life, that her bright twinkling eyes, pretty face, and shapely figure were his to cherish. He hurriedly placed his bag and the flowers that he had bought down by the door and pulled her to him, holding her tight before allowing his hands to explore the heavenly contours of her body a little. He just needed to remind himself that she was real.

When he had satiated his need to feel and breathe her in a little, he opened his eyes and looked over her shoulder into the small entrance hall. The open door at the other side of the hall revealed a large pine table with varying styles of wooden chairs, adorned with brightly coloured cushions. He closed the front door, and she took his hand and led him into the dining space and open plan kitchen. The place had a warm and welcoming feel to it even though the wood burning stove in the corner of the room was not lit. The room smelt of incense and wood smoke and the low wooden beams and carefully chosen ornaments and pictures created a lovely atmosphere. He noted that she was tidy like him and he approved of her ability to create a lovely home.

"Where is the bedroom?" he asked with a cheeky grin.

"I'll show you that in a minute," she replied as she turned and filled the kettle at the large white sink.

After she had arranged the flowers with care in a tall, slender vase, they sat at the kitchen table drinking herb tea. He made sure that they sat close enough so that he could hold her hand and reach over to kiss her soft cheek occasionally while they took it in turns to catch up on the events of the week while they had been apart. She was always excited by her studies and told him in detail about the latest assignment she was working on and a few anecdotes from her days at the cafe. He did his best to listen attentively, but his mind sometimes wandered when his gaze fell upon the delicate nape of her neck, or an inch or two of succulent thigh momentarily revealed when she arranged her position on the chair. God, he was hungry for her. How could it be that he was always so hungry for her?

After a while, she showed him around the rest of her charming little cottage. When they arrived at the bedroom, he quickly put his bag down and, catching her unawares, gently pushed her back onto the bed. To his dismay, there was a disturbing clunk as a couple of slats under the mattress became displaced. He was a little embarrassed and apologised, but she reassured him, in between fits of giggles, that it could easily be remedied. The next ten minutes were spent repositioning the offending slats and, with the moment gone and time moving all too quickly, there was just enough time for her to get ready before they needed to leave for their evening out. They had tickets to attend a storytelling performance in a nearby town.

She drove them the short distance, and they found a parking place close to the venue. They both knew how to do the magic manifesting trick that meant there was always a parking space for them. She commented that it was a bit of a rough area and he squeezed her hand softly as they made their way to the venue, to reassure her that she was safe with him by her side.

As always, she looked stunning, and he felt an inch or two taller than usual as he walked proudly beside her.

On arriving, he opened the door for her, and they entered a small, busy room with rows of chairs crammed together. At the back was a small wholefood café and they joined the queue to order their food. Apart from their visits to restaurants, it was the first time that they had been out in public together. He loved being with her, even though he was unsure whether the evening would be to his liking. He had decided that he would try anything that she wanted to show his commitment. As long as he was with her, he didn't mind. The food was good, and they talked as best they could amongst the din of all the other people in the small room. After a while, the storytellers were ready to begin, and three young men walked onto the makeshift stage at the front. He felt a small pang of jealousy knowing that she was giving her full attention to other men and he hoped that she did not find them too attractive. He couldn't believe he was having such a crazy thought and quickly dismissed it. As if reading his mind, she took his hand and placed it on her lap.

The evening began to unfold before them, and soon he was lost in the magic of the stories. He relaxed and allowed himself to enjoy the richness of the atmosphere. In what seemed like no time at all the room was full of applause, the stories were all told, and they made their way to the door. She had thoroughly enjoyed the show, and he had been pleasantly surprised at how much he had, too. Not being very sociable, he had become a bit of a hermit before she had arrived in his life and he was aware that one of the gifts she brought was her enthusiasm to have as many different experiences as possible. As they drove back to her home, they talked about their favourite parts of the stories they had heard and about the magic and power of storytelling.

On arriving back at her cottage, he could already feel the excitement rising in his body as she closed the front door behind them. She knew what he was thinking and, after they had removed their jackets, she sauntered slowly over to him, smiling, and stood in front of him with their toes almost touching. He paused momentarily to fully enjoy the view, looking lovingly into her eyes. He was reminded of how he loved the way that she could hold his gaze as she looked unashamedly into his appreciative eyes.

Then their lips were together, gently and softly at first. As he kissed her delicately, the feel of the tip of her tongue against the inside of his upper lip awoke the dragon that was already stirring within him. He grabbed her around the waist and pulled her firmly towards him. With his other hand, he gripped a generous handful of her ample buttocks, the muscles in his arm tensed so that she was held tightly in his embrace. She tasted delicious as always and his passion sored at an alarming rate, facilitated by her skill in quickly undoing his belt and sliding her hand inside his jeans.

She fondled him roughly with her cool, slim, delicate fingers. His tongue probed and explored inside the sultry wetness of her succulent mouth, while he held her even more tightly. Waves of delicious energy surged up his spine, and his hands prized their way between their bodies to feel the curves of her breasts. Unexpectedly, she pushed him away, just enough so that she could kneel down before him. In no time at all his trousers and shorts were around his ankles and she had taken him into her eager mouth. His head fell back, and his long brown hair hung limply down his back as he moaned and sighed with delight. Every now and then he would take a handful of her hair and pull her head back just enough so that he could look into her happy eyes while her mouth could still perpetuate the pleasure as she sucked and licked him tenderly, and then passionately, and then tenderly again.

Over and over again he whispered, "Thank you, thank you, thank you."

When it felt as if he could not endure the ecstasy any longer, he raised her up so that she stood before him and he could look lovingly into her eyes once again. Her hair was already wild and unkempt, and her lips glistened with wetness from her mouth.

It was his turn, and he crouched down before her. His hands found their way up her thighs and eased her knickers down, and she stepped out of them obediently. He turned her around until her back was now against the wooden table and then lifted her up so that she was sat perched on the edge. He pulled her scarlet skirt up around her thighs to reveal a beautiful contrast of her pale skin against the edge of the black lace at the top of her elasticated stockings.

Again, their mouths met while their tongues gladly endured the drenched sweetness that bathed them. He waited as long as he was able before he slid himself gently inside her silky slipperiness. Waves of white fire rippled through his body, as it was her turn to moan with gratitude at the arrival of what she had been waiting for.

Her delicate fingers became talons as she clawed at his back, while her head fell back, begging his mouth to lick and kiss her erogenous zone at the nape of her delicate neck.

She was his, and his body moved accordingly, his hips dancing rhythmically to a silent song of awe and gratitude for being alive in a body able to experience such pleasure. There were no thoughts, only the moment immersed in waves of bliss.

Forcing his mouth from hers for a moment, he whispered to her "O my God you are so beautiful."

The rise in volume of her gasps aroused him more and more, and he thrust deeper and harder inside her until her gasps became screams and her body began to convulse over and over again. As she trembled and moved with the kundalini energy, he held himself still inside her and looked on, smiling at her wild, untamed beauty.

Then, they held each other closely and tenderly for a while, in the quietness of her kitchen. He carefully slipped himself from inside her, took her hand and led her upstairs. He removed his shirt while she slipped out of her skirt. He pointed to the bed. "Lay on your back."

She tilted her head in a coquettish manner and looked at him with raised eyebrows.

"Please," he added.

She did as she was asked and in an instant, he was inside her again. Her hands gripped the headboard behind her, and he slid his hands underneath her buttocks and held her while he pushed himself over and over inside her deliciousness until the waves of fire inside him rushed to release. As he did so, he lifted himself until his arms were locked, back arched, head thrown back, while an unearthly roar arose from deep within him. Waves of ecstatic energy coursed up his spine and the loud sound quickly quietened to sobs and moans as he struggled to contain the intensity of the feelings he felt in his body. Tears started falling from his eyes.

Spent and exhausted, he collapsed onto her naked chest while his lungs did their best to inhale enough air. She ran her fingers through his hair and gently caressed his sweat-drenched back; laid there together, they were totally connected and at peace.

Once he could muster the energy, he removed himself from her and kissed her belly, as he always did before lying beside her. Then, unexpectedly, laughter began arising from within him. There was no reason or thoughts that initiated the laughter. Nevertheless, he found himself gripped by wave after wave of giggling fits that intensified uncontrollably until his eyes streamed with new tears and his stomach muscles ached. He was at the mercy of the energy and was literally powerless to do anything about it. Every now and then he would try to compose himself, but usually, the expression on her face was enough to set him off again. After about five minutes it passed, and he glanced at her to see her looking at him with a mixed look of concern and amusement. She asked what he had been laughing about, but he really didn't know. He was just laughing. It was another one of those beautiful and unusual things that appeared to be the result of their kundalini energy. He rather liked to call it magic!

CHAPTER 8

The sky was grey and the weather a little chilly for May, but it didn't matter because today was the day they were heading off on their romantic adventure to Devon.

She arrived at his flat promptly at the agreed time, and he loaded her bag into the boot of his car along with his own. They set off and were soon on the motorway heading south. Normally, a three-and-a-half-hour drive would have seemed like a long time to be in a car, but he was delighted to have so much time together. As they talked, the time and miles sped by. Occasionally, he would take her hand and place it on his lap so that there was some physical connection.

Once they had left the busyness of the motorway, they found a place to stop beside the road for a picnic. The sun was shining now, and they sat on the fragrant grass munching crisps and the sandwiches that she had lovingly prepared. Afterward, there was time for a kiss and a cuddle, though she was a little self-conscious of the passing cars.

"Let them see us," he said. "After all, what will they see but two people loving each other."

She relaxed a little and allowed him to enjoy the sweetness of her lips and mouth, though his hands were firmly guided away from areas that were out of bounds in such a public place.

They returned to the car, and she decided to take a little cat nap while they traveled and, arranging a small blanket from the back seat of the car around her, she closed her eyes. He was left to his own thoughts as the car found its way along the winding roads as the Devon countryside became more and more unspoiled and natural.

He pondered his feelings for her and decided that the intensity of what he was feeling must be love. He knew that he had been in love before, but this was something very new. He was confused by the rich tapestry of emotions that she evoked in him and was acutely aware that some of them were highly uncomfortable. The video about twin flames came to mind, and then he remembered the mysterious words that she had heard. 'Bring him home.'

The more he thought about it, the more he became convinced that there was something divine at play, that she had been sent so that he might realise the full extent and depth of love. Of course, this meant that he would have to dissolve any of the barriers within himself that blocked love. And he was resigned to the fact there was still more healing to be done around his mother wound, which was the most obvious barrier. He believed that every being is the embodiment of love and that the journey of ascension or healing is about reawakening to our true divinity as love incarnate. Nevertheless, he made up his mind there and then that when the moment presented itself, while they were away together, he would speak to her for the first time of his human love for her.

And then the mind came rushing in with a predictable fear-based question. 'What if she did not feel the same?' He knew that he desperately wanted her to echo back the same words to him but, reminded himself that this was not a

Hollywood movie. He just needed to speak his truth without any attachment to her response; in doing so, he would be honouring himself.

They arrived at the small town by the sea and spent quite a while looking for the cottage. The satnav was most unhelpful and, as the sun was now shining, they were keen to find their temporary home, stretch their legs and enjoy a walk on the beach before it got too late. In the end, they found the cottage and were delighted with the warm, friendly ambiance. He carried the bags hurriedly inside and after a quick change of clothes she was ready to accompany him down to the beach.

Although the late afternoon breeze was a little chilly, he loved the feel of the cool sand between his toes, and they walked hand in hand together talking, laughing and taking in their surroundings. Other couples were walking, too, and old men with dogs that were intermittently chasing sticks or sniffing each other. Children paddled in the foamy water while anxious parents barked instructions and warnings. Above them, the cotton wool clouds meandered lazily by, and all was well.

After they had sufficiently stretched their legs and had their fill of the seaside, they took in three large full breaths of the ocean air together before saying goodbye to the beach and made their way back to the cottage. While he unpacked their bags, she prepared a small banquet of cheeses that she had bought, along with bread, salad, olives, and chorizo. The chilled bottle of prosecco from the fridge, which had been thoughtfully left for them by the cottage owner, was opened and they settled down to the first proper meal of their first holiday together.

When the table had been cleared away, they sat together for a while on the sofa and watched a video that she had wanted to see on YouTube. They snuggled up close, sipping their newly refilled glasses of bubbly.

They talked a little about the video when it had finished and, occasionally, the now familiar little tremors would move through her. Although it was still relatively early, she announced that she was tired and ready for bed. He was used to her being tired, mainly because she was menopausal and her sleep was often disturbed, and partly because of her extremely busy life. He also suspected that the kundalini energy she was experiencing might be responsible, too, as it was working its healing magic.

He had researched the phenomenon a bit in the last few weeks and understood her tremors to be the result of a recalibration of the nervous system to adapt to the vast increase in circulating energy she must be experiencing. Not only was he charmed by the magical nature of her shivers and trembles when they arrived, but he was also now additionally contented by the knowledge that healing energy was coursing through her.

For a fleeting moment, he thought that she might be too worn out to make love but, was reassured by quickly reminding himself that this had never happened yet. This night was to be no different and, as far as libido was concerned, they appeared to be perfectly matched. Guided by his intuition and her subtle signals, their time under the covers was softer and more gentle than usual. He thought she seemed a little less present and their nakedness, albeit delicious, did not deliver him to the usual depth and intensity of intimacy that he had become accustomed to. When the energy had settled, they rested together in the unfamiliar bed. For a while, she lay with her head on his chest and his arm around her. He loved those moments. Her body trembled a little every now and then, but they hardly noticed it anymore. A kiss on the cheek and a soft "Goodnight darling" informed him that she was ready for sleep.

He dismissed the by now familiar and unwelcome thoughts that arose while he lay awake in the bed next to her. He listened to her breath rising and falling. Occasionally, he glanced at her blonde tresses, still visible in the half-light, strewn untidily across her pillow, as she lay on her side in her usual sleeping position with her back to him. He shuffled over and spooned her, enjoying the feeling of her soft, ample buttocks against his upper thighs and eventually he too fell asleep.

THE NEXT MORNING the sun was shining and, though neither of them had slept particularly well in the strange bed, they decided to take a walk. However, the simple task of deciding where to go became an issue. Usually, he was happy to go wherever she wanted, but on this morning, things were different. He wanted to just set off on and see where they ended up while she was intent on following a route laid out by the Devon walkers' book that she had brought along. They couldn't decide how long they wanted to walk for because some time relaxing on the beach was also high on their priorities for the day. She wanted to drive to a starting place as laid out by the map, while he was tired of driving from the previous day and just wanted to head out from the cottage. After some debate, they reached a compromise and set off on foot to follow a guided walk along the nearby cliff tops. He was aware that his head was a little unclear from the previous night's wine and put his irritation with her down to a slight hangover.

But, as they left the town and climbed the steep hill up to the cliffs, it became very apparent that something was not right. Usually, they would walk hand in hand, but she seemed to be walking deliberately slow. She said that she was tired, but it seemed that the more he slowed down to match her pace, the slower she walked. Eventually, frustrated and impatient, he let go of her hand, and they walked with him in front and her behind. The physical distance between them only accentuated the disconnect that he felt from her. The usual togetherness was not there. A sense that she was no longer fully with him on some level stimulated his impatience and insecurity even more.

By the time they were on the cliff top path, she was quite a way behind. He decided that he would just walk at his pace and after a while, he sat down to wait for her. A few minutes passed, and there was still no sign of her, so he stood up and backtracked. He rounded the bend, and to his dismay, he saw her in the distance, stood still with her arms outstretched gazing out across the sea.

She looked as beautiful as ever, but the feelings inside him became more acute as he muttered unkind comments under his breath.

He set off again along the path unsure of what he was doing until he found a smooth piece of grass to lie down on, in an attempt to center himself and let go of the troublesome emotions that filled him. By the time she arrived, he had been unsuccessful in his attempts, and he barked out "What is wrong with you?"

"Nothing," she said. "I am just tired, and I stopped to feel the wind in my hair and take in the beauty of the place."

"But there is something else. Something doesn't feel right. What's wrong?" he demanded.

She insisted that everything was fine, and he had no choice but to believe her. He apologised for his behaviour, concluding that it must just be him, but the distance between them remained. They decided to turn around. She was tired, the sun was getting hot, and the idea of putting an end to what was meant to have been a romantic stroll was appealing to them both.

By the time they had cooked and eaten lunch back at the cottage, the sky had clouded over, and they decided to visit a little picturesque fishing village a short drive away along the coast. She wanted to buy some gifts for a couple of friends and, as was usually the case, he was happy for her to take the lead. After the morning's shenanigans, it seemed like a good idea.

The town was pretty enough, but he was quickly bored with the shops she wanted to visit. Shopping was not his thing, and he just couldn't shake off the uncomfortable feeling. She looked so lovely in her summer dress and denim jacket, but it was as if she was behind a glass screen and he couldn't reach her. At one point, as they walked along the pier, he asked if she would stop a moment so that he could take a photo of her. He wanted to capture her beauty but, to his surprise, she said no and walked ahead to escape the camera. He was perplexed; this did nothing to reassure him that all was well.

As they walked towards the restaurants on the seafront, she explained that she had reservations about having her picture taken. He did his best to dismiss what seemed to him like a deliberate attempt at being awkward.

It took forever to choose a place to eat. He was happy to eat wherever she wanted as decisions were not always his strong point. He was the sort of person that struggled to choose from the menu; no matter what he ordered everyone else's meal often seemed to be better! This time, she wanted him to decide where they ate, and he was a little overwhelmed with the amount of options, and it became her turn to be irritated by him. After some deliberation, he chose a pub where they could eat outside and enjoy the sea view.

While they ate the distance between them closed a little. Their surroundings were picturesque, and it was their first time eating out al fresco together. The holiday feeling returned a little with full bellies and the lovely seaside setting.

By the time they got back to their holiday home the light was fading, and soon they were in bed. By the time he had returned from the bathroom, she was reading her book. But a few kisses to the back of her neck persuaded her to put it down, and soon they were again making love. Her kisses were as tender as ever, and he brought his usual awareness to pleasing her, hoping that intimacy and passion would dissolve any distance that remained between them.

He was pleased to have her all to himself for so much time, yet the holiday was not panning out quite as he had hoped. He had consciously decided not to have any wine, thinking that this was perhaps to blame for his unsettled emotional state. Hopefully, tomorrow they would both awaken feeling refreshed. As sleep took him, he placated his anxious thoughts and reassured himself with those mysterious words 'Bring him home.' Everything would be fine as she was going to bring him home. He knew that they had not arrived home, there was more fear to be dissolved from around his heart center, and so their time together was not over. And after all, tomorrow would be a new day.

AGAIN, THEY WERE blessed with the weather and decided to spend some time on the beach in the morning in case it clouded over in the afternoon like the previous day. To his dismay, he realised that he had forgotten to pack his swimming trunks. She seemed more bothered than he was about this and he defended his ineptitude by insisting that he would be fine in his boxer shorts. Nobody would ever know the difference.

With a picnic, books, and towels they headed down to the beach and found a spot not too close to the other folk who were keen to feel the sun's warm kiss against their pale skin, also. He strolled down to the sea and left her with her book. The water was cold, yet he waded in, intent on making the most of his beach holiday. As he walked back up the beach, he wanted her to be looking out for him, watching him as he returned, but she was lost in her book. A sprinkle of cold water from his wet hair brought her momentarily from her other world and then she disappeared again into the pages. He lay on his back and felt the sun slowly warm him. When he was almost dry, he rolled over onto his side so that he could take in the lovely semi-naked view of her. She looked divine!

"Darling," he said.

She lowered her book and glanced over at him, shielding the sun from her eyes with her hand.

"I love you," he said, looking directly into her blue eyes.

He noticed her expression before any words left her lips and it alarmed him. It probably only lasted for a second, but he saw it. It was a look of concern rather than joy, and his heart sank a little. Of course, he wanted her to say it in return. But, instead, the look of concern quickly changed to a sweet smile, and she replied "That's a really lovely thing to say. Thank you."

She allowed him to kiss her lightly on the lips, but there was no softness or yielding in it. He lay beside her and caressed her a little, and she returned to her book. He reminded himself that he was not attached to her response and that he had spoken from his heart. It was clear that she did not feel the same way because if she had, she would have told him so, but he reassured himself with memories of the passion between them when they made love and felt certain that in time she would fall in love with him, too. He quickly erased the image of her initial concerned expression from his mind.

That evening, back at the cottage he cooked them dahl and rice. Afterward, they cuddled up together and watched a movie on the laptop. As it ended, he noticed that the sun was going down and as the sky was clear he suggested that they go down to watch the sun set behind the ocean. He felt it would be a lovely thing to share. However, she declined the invitation, saying that she was feeling tired and a little drunk.

She suggested that he go alone, and he could see that she had made up her mind. He wondered about staying with her because he didn't want to go alone, but he set off anyway, with disappointment and an acute sense of rejection rising in him. He could feel the effect of the red wine as he walked alone briskly and realised that he was a little drunker than he had realised. The sun was dipping fast, and he jogged the last bit down to the beach. He caught the last of the large orange orb sinking into the horizon, but it was not beautiful. He was angry with her. He felt desolate and alone. If everything were fine, then surely, she would have made an effort to come with him. Didn't he always try to be considerate of her wishes and needs?

When he returned, the sofa was empty, and he found her in bed with her book.

"I'm having an early night. I am so tired," she said lightly as he stood in the doorway.

"Okay," he replied and closed the door.

But it wasn't okay. It was far from okay. He felt horrible. Something was not right, and he knew it, but he tried to convince himself that he was being ridiculous and making a big deal about nothing.

The distraction of the laptop did little to ease his troubled mind. He so wanted to make love to her, to be close, to be intimate, to make everything feel good again. He knew that, to some extent, physical intimacy was a temporary fix for the loneliness and disconnection that he sometimes felt inside. But, for some reason, the fear was stronger this evening. He didn't feel he could speak to her about what was on his mind in case she denied that anything was wrong. He didn't dare to return to the bedroom and touch her in case she declined his advances and triggered the growing sense of rejection inside him.

He sat for a while with his inner turmoil and eventually, he made his way to their bed, tired and distraught. She was asleep, but he couldn't help himself, and he caressed her back and thigh hoping to rouse her from her slumber.

"I'm so tired," she mumbled and pushed his hand away.

He lay on his back as far over the other side of the bed as possible. How could she sleep while he was feeling so distraught and upset? It was so painful to feel her so close to him and yet feel that something had closed inside her; it was if she was a million miles away.

He tried to sleep, he tried to quiet his raging mind. He tried to feel the fullness of the emotions that felt like they would drown him, but it was hopeless. After what seemed like an eternity, he got up and climbed into the single bed in the spare room and lay there, allowing the feelings to wash over him. He waited for their intensity to diminish, but they didn't. Finally, he put a movie on to distract himself. Although his eyes and ears followed the story that unfolded on the screen before him, the wretched feeling inside him only grew. Every now and then he would go to the door of the other bedroom in the hope that she might be awake and available to talk, but each time he went, she was fast asleep. This only angered him more.

When he could restrain himself no longer, he climbed back into the bed with her and shook her awake.

"We need to talk," he said. "I am in so much pain."

She turned to face him, but she was not there. The woman who he cared so much about was gone.

They argued, and she explained that she had just been tired and didn't want to see the sunset. They could see it another time. But he felt that there was more to it; something just didn't feel right.

"This is the first time that we have not made love before going to sleep, you know?"

"You should have said," she countered "I would have made love."

He felt foolish and ashamed that he had not dared to ask her clearly because of his fear of rejection. Perhaps she was right, and he was making it all up in his mind.

"I don't know what's wrong with you. I don't know if I can do this anymore," she added.

"What does that mean?" he demanded. "Can't do what? You mean you can't do 'us'?"

"I don't know. Let's talk in the morning," she suggested.

She turned her back on him, and it was clear that the conversation was over.

He returned to the other bed as the light began to filter in from outside in one last desperate attempt to find solace and the peace of sleep, but it was not to be.

He didn't understand what was happening to him, he couldn't see anything clearly anymore. His emotional response seemed ridiculously out of proportion to what had happened; it was just a sunset, but he couldn't snap out of it. All he could feel was a dull, wretched ache in his chest and nausea in his stomach.

As the screeching of the freshly risen seagulls reached what seemed like a deafening crescendo, he couldn't control himself anymore. He stormed into the room where she lay sleeping.

"We have to leave. I can't stay here with you when you are so closed off and distant. It's just too painful."

"What, now?" she replied with an exasperated look on her face.

"Yes. I am going to pack and load the car."

He set about gathering their belongings. Before long she was also out of bed and packing her things.

As the sun rose, they drove back along the roads that had so recently promised such delights. At least she was awake now, and he could express himself, but he found himself ranting and raving at her. His words were accusatory and unkind and cutting and, though he tried to be calm, the emotion inside him was like a torrent of lava that had to find its release from a volcano of pain inside. He begged her to tell him what was wrong, what was going on in her mind. She continued to counter his attacks with calm reason and logic, insisting that nothing was wrong and that he was just being ridiculous, but he couldn't really hear what she was saying. Her cool and distant demeanor only fueled his desperation to reach her; the more desperate he became, the more she withdrew behind a thick icy wall.

After a while, she couldn't take any more of the fear and anger that he projected at her.

"You have to stop talking at me," she pleaded. "It's like a hammer bashing against my skull. I can't take it."

He apologised and fell silent, trying his best to calm the raging in his mind and body by focusing on the road as the motorway raced by in a grey blur.

But, in silence, with no outlet for his pain, the pressure inside began to mount. Tears streamed down his face, and his lungs began to take in and exhale huge breaths of air. With a will of its own, his chest rose and fell time and time again until he noticed that his hands and feet were beginning to go numb from the over oxygenation of his blood. He knew he needed to stop driving and began looking desperately for a sign for a service station.

"I can't feel my hands or feet."

He tried to regulate his breathing until, at last, they arrived at a service station.

He parked hurriedly, threw the door open and ran for a small grassy mound speckled with young rowan trees. He knew he had to be on the earth and instinctively removed his shoes and socks and lay on his back, still breathing heavily. Then the floodgates really opened, and a fresh torrent of tears fell from his eyes as his body convulsed with the severity of the emotional release. He wailed and moaned like a traumatised child, alone, scared, and abandoned.

Then he noticed that she was kneeling by his side and she took his hand in hers and whispered soothing words to him until the tears eventually began to lessen and his breathing became more rhythmic and shallower.

"I have something to tell you," she said.

From his resting place on the earth, he looked up at her beautiful face as she began to speak of a dark time from her past that, until now, had remained a secret. Tears began to roll down her cheeks as she told him of another chapter of her life that had been infused with pain and suffering. She explained that she had grown up in a very restrictive religious community, which at times conflicted with her values. Later, as a wife and a mother, she discovered that certain individuals had colluded to hush up sexual misconduct within the community. Being a woman of integrity, she spoke out and repeatedly challenged this wrongdoing until she became unpopular with the community leaders. Rumours were spread about her in an attempt to cover things up and, within a short space of time, she was totally ostracized from almost everyone that she had known her whole life. Suddenly, she found herself going through a divorce, totally isolated and alone. Perhaps she had thought he would judge her in some way, but her vulnerability in the moment only endeared her to him more.

He sat up, and they were together, wrapped in each other's arms as their tears blended and trickled down their necks.

"Why didn't you tell me before?" he asked, exasperated.

He had known that something was not right, that there was a distance between them, and this had made him feel insecure and shut out.

She explained that she had intended to tell him, but because things were not great between them, she just couldn't find the right moment.

"It doesn't make any difference to how I feel about you, darling," he said, stroking her long blonde hair.

It all made sense now; this was why he had felt that she was so unavailable to him.

She said nothing and they lay down on the grass side by side, with her hand in his, looking up at the sky, breathing together.

When they were ready, he put his shoes and socks back on, and they returned to the car, homeward bound. He felt a little calmer as they drove.

"I need some space to come to terms with everything that has happened," she said.

He agreed. It would be a good idea for her to have a walk in the hills, and perhaps he could prepare them some food. He knew that she didn't have to be back at work for two days and he felt that everything would be different now that there were no secrets between them.

"No," she said. "I need more time than that."

He felt the panic rising in him again. He needed a clear time frame, he needed some hope that they were not over, that she would come back.

"I don't know," she said. "I just know that I need time. Let's say two weeks."

Her words pierced his already tender heart and, though he tried to get her to change her mind, it was already made up, and she would not budge. How could she possibly need two weeks? How was he supposed to handle so much time not knowing if he would see her again or not? He felt it would be easier to finish it there and then, but he couldn't bring himself to say the words.

The pain in his chest that had settled down returned with a vengeance. He desperately wanted to get out of the car, but he knew that every mile closer to his home meant that she would be leaving, and he didn't know if he would ever see her again. In that moment he loved and hated her in equal measure.

The little blue car arrived back on his drive, and he unloaded her bag from the back and placed it beside her own car. She stood as if waiting for a hug from him, but he couldn't. He just couldn't, it was too painful. He staggered up the drive with his bag; his legs felt full of lead, and his heart was heavy with sadness. He wanted to turn and say something kind to her, but his legs wouldn't stop, and he couldn't look back.

CHAPTER 9

I t was good to be home, but that was the only thing that felt good.

The tears began to fall yet again, and he dragged his body around his flat, doing his best to keep busy by unpacking his bag and putting things away. When it was done, he returned to his car to collect the rest of his holiday belongings, foolishly hoping that her car would be there. Maybe she had changed her mind, and they would be able to talk and find some resolution and comfort, but he should have known by now that talking was not her way. The empty space and the tire marks on the ground where her car had been taunted him.

When there were no more simple tasks that he could busy himself with he collapsed on the sofa and cried out in desperation. "O God help me! I can't handle this."

He couldn't understand what was happening to him and why the pain he felt was so excruciating. It compared to some extent with what he had experienced on leaving his wife and children ten years earlier, but he had only known this woman for four months. The words 'Bring him home' entered his awareness but in his distraught state, they no longer made any sense.

Then his mobile rang. It was one of his best male friends, and he answered it.

He spilled out the story of recent events while his patient friend listened and did his best to console him, but he was passed consoling. Half into the phone and half into the room, he heard himself wail. "I want my mummy!"

He immediately felt embarrassed by what he had heard himself say, but his friend did his best to reassure him and offered some kind and empathic advice. He had only called to reschedule their meeting, and after a short while, he had to go. As the phone call ended, he was sharply catapulted back to his room with his aloneness and desolation.

He paced around over and over, stopping only to roll a cigarette, which he smoked by the open patio doors. Apart from the brief respite that the numbing nicotine offered, he endured wave after wave of grief and terror, all the time berating himself for his ridiculously dramatic behaviour.

He wanted to walk on the hills, but he was too weak. Although his stomach was empty, it also felt nauseous, and the idea of eating something was not an option. As time wore on, he crawled into his bed with his laptop to try and find some distraction from the intensity of his ragged emotional state. The movie only vaguely distracted him from what he was feeling, and his ears pricked up at every sound outside with the futile hope that she had returned to him.

AT SOME POINT, sleep had overtaken him. When he awoke, just a few hours later, the pain in his chest was just as acute. Memories of what had happened the previous day came flooding back in to cut him mercilessly.

He showered and dressed and made himself a cup of tea, adding a large spoon of honey by way of some palatable sustenance. After too many cigarettes he drove the short distance up to the hills. The walk felt like a death march, and he plodded on, stopping briefly at the place where they had often sat and laughed and cuddled together. But the hills worked their magic, and as he neared his car, he remembered the words that had spilled from his mouth when he had been on the phone to his friend the previous day. At that moment, he saw through the emotional fog. This intense experience was clearly related to the death of his mother. As thoughts came into focus in his tired mind, he began to make a little sense of what was happening. He decided that he had to go to the grave of his mother. He needed ceremony, an event or something with which he could use to draw a line in the sand and free himself from the shackles of his past once and for all.

Finding his mother's grave would not be straight forward, though. He knew she was buried somewhere in the south of England, but he did not know exactly where, as he had only been there once, over twenty years earlier. Why had he not been back? He wasn't sure, but he had an intensely strong knowing that this was something that he needed to do.

He drove recklessly down the hill towards home. When he arrived, he phoned his father who lived in Spain, but there was no response. Who else might know where she was buried? He tried his eldest brother and both sisters; again, no one answered his calls.

Then he called his aunty and uncle who lived in Australia. They had taken care of him for a year after his mother had died until his father had remarried and the family had been reunited. To his great relief, they answered his call. Although he found some satisfaction in sharing his revelation that he needed to visit his mother's grave in the hope that it would bring closure, they did not know exactly where the grave was.

By this time, he was feeling an increasing sense of urgency in achieving his goal. If it brought some relief and healing, it had to be done. He wanted to do it now, today before the pressures of life limited his time. He hadn't wanted to call his stepmother because it felt as if this was something that had nothing to do with her, but he was desperate to find his mother's final resting place. He decided to call, and fortunately, she picked up the phone. He broke down in tears again as he told her as briefly as possible what was happening, doing his best not to alarm her. But she had no idea where the grave was. He pressed her, asking who else might know. It was vital that he found out today.

She suggested that an old friend of the family might know and she gave him a mobile number to call. To his relief, his call was answered, and at last, he was given the name of the village and church where he would find what he was seeking.

He was like a man possessed, and the busy urgency of his mission was a welcome respite from the dull ache that plagued his heart. Hurriedly, he threw some fruit, a big bottle of spring water and some candles and incense for his mum's ceremony into a bag. The satnav told him that it would take around three hours to get there. It didn't matter to him; he would have driven all day. He knew the time was right to do what he probably should have done a long time before. His pain was an invitation to bring closure to this trauma that he had experienced at such a tender age, and he just had to get to the grave and do what needed to be done. Though he wasn't quite sure what that was yet, he trusted that all would be clear when he arrived.

The drive was a vague blur. In his eagerness, he drove too fast, knuckles white on the steering wheel. The car stereo was at full volume and its blaring music, along with the noise from the open windows, washed over him. He felt crazed, and wild thoughts raced through his mind. How ironic it would be if he were to be killed on the road while on his way to lay his demons to rest at the graveside of his mother. It was a frenzied and unlikely sort of pilgrimage!

Ultimately, after what seemed like a long time and in no time at all, he arrived at his destination and parked the car on the side of the quiet village road in Hampshire. He had a photo with him of himself and his siblings at the graveside to help him find her grave, which had been taken when he had last visited.

It didn't take him long to find it in the small graveyard. Though the headstone was new when the photo was taken, it was now weather-worn and grey with lichen. He was pleased to see that it was under the shade of a beautiful old yew tree. Before approaching he removed his shoes and socks, then moved slowly forward.

He read the engraved words and was shocked to realise that he had not previously known the date of her birth or death. Perhaps this was indicative of how her passing had never really been discussed as he grew up or during his adult life.

He spoke to her as if she were there before him, but in a soft voice, as if she was not in the best of health. She said nothing back, but in the yew tree, a raven cawed. High above in the distance, he heard a buzzard's cry.

He walked around the small churchyard, gathering a few wildflowers and some fir cones with which he decorated the foot of the grave. He lit a candle and the incense that he had brought and lay down on the warm, damp grass beside her. As he did so he noticed an easing in his chest and, as he lay there in conversation with his mother, he found some peace.

After a long while, he sat up and cut his index finger with a penknife that he took from his pocket. He squeezed out a small drop of blood which he allowed to fall onto the grass. He wanted to leave a part of him with her so that their bodies could in some way meet in the earth.

He didn't really believe in death as an ending. He preferred to see it that she had left her body and that her essence was eternal and was somehow with him on that day and always. He asked her to help him let go, once and for all, the grief that still, after nearly fifty years, was with him. He told her that he knew she had to leave him when he was a baby and that he understood that it was necessary to guide and shape his own life journey. She listened respectfully without interrupting.

When he had shared everything, his tender heart had to offer he lay quietly for a while, enjoying the calm that engulfed him and the buzz of insects and the hum of cars, occasionally passing by along the sleepy lane.

He ate his banana and savoured the coolness of the water.

Before leaving, he took a few photos. When he was done, he replaced his socks and shoes and said goodbye with a loving kiss planted on the top of the headstone. It was all rather surreal.

ON THE JOURNEY back home, he noticed that the further he got from the churchyard the more his temporary feeling of peace ebbed away. As he arrived, his dull aching heart became his companion once again.

He lay awake in bed wondering how he was going to manage twelve more days alone. How could she possibly need two weeks? Was she aware of the torture he was enduring? He was versed well enough in matters of grief to know that all he could do was take one day at a time. Yes, that was it. He was grieving the loss of his mother through this experience. He saw it clearly for a moment before the insight was engulfed again by the thick emotional fog.

There was a strange kind of comfort in knowing that at least he had a few meetings to attend the next day that would disturb the monotony of the feelings he carried inside him. He didn't want to see anyone, yet without any distraction, his aloneness seemed almost unbearable.

He wondered what she was doing now and if she was missing him. God, how he hoped that she was; even though at the same time he wished her no malice. He had decided not to get in touch with her. He didn't want her to know the mess he was in. He preferred to give her the impression that he was fine without her and, anyway, he knew that one wrong word or emoticon in a message could potentially add to his mind's torture. His thoughts were already challenging enough as he tried to get a grip on reality and a cold, aloof message from her would launch him into a deeper pain and anxiety than he was already feeling. He only had twelve more days to endure; surely things would get easier now that he had made peace with his mother.

Sleep was again limited, and he awoke much too early for his liking with the long day menacingly stretched out in front of him. His morning walk on the hills brought some ease, though his body felt weak since he had still not managed to eat anything more than a little fruit and some yogurt. His main source of sustenance was lots of milky red-bush tea with honey. His throat was sore from smoking too many cigarettes, and he felt like a zombie, somehow detached from the world in which he moved through.

Between the day's work commitments, he went shopping, hoping that he would not see anyone that he knew. He bought some more fruit and some soup as it seemed that this was the sort of food that was most palatable; he had to try and keep up his strength.

But strength was something that seemed to be in short supply. In a moment of weakness, he sent her a message asking if they could speak. The couple of hours waiting for her response seemed like an eternity. When it arrived, it took him more deeply back into his pain. It wasn't that she was unkind, she merely stated that she needed more time and that she would be in touch as soon as she had found some clarity. The bit that really hurt was that she said she was having a lovely time being in nature and reconnecting with herself, which she had lost touch with in recent months. It wasn't that he didn't want her to be having a nice time, but it didn't seem to make sense that she could be having such a nice time when he was suffering as he was.

At times he was tempted to revert to his old addiction and buy some cannabis. It had always been his crutch in times of emotional challenge, but he was resolute that this time would be different. This time he would face whatever he needed to face without hiding behind a stoned haze. He would feel whatever he needed to feel so that once and for all the shadow of his mother's death would cease to haunt him. The trauma had been hidden away for long enough in the depths of his psyche, and it was time for it to be banished, transformed, healed.

The mystic poet Rumi's words found him, and he printed them out and pinned them beside his bed. 'The wound is the place where the light enters. Stay with it.'

And so, he did his best to stay with all that he was feeling. He paced around his flat for hours, repeating Rumi's words over and over. It took the edge off the ordeal.

Seemingly by chance, a friend sent him a link to some music that he had not heard before. The musician's words seemed to express much of his own feelings and philosophy, and he played it repeatedly at full volume, sometimes screaming along at the top of his voice. It gave him some relief, but it was limited and all too fleeting.

He phoned a few close friends and shared his heart with them, and their kindness always brought a little temporary comfort. But all too often once he was back with himself, his thoughts would return to her. Would he ever see her again? Was it really over? It was the not knowing that made it extra difficult. He knew that if they were finished, he could begin getting over her and he thought about ending it himself. But the thought didn't last long. It wasn't what he wanted and, anyway, it would be a cowardly thing to do.

EACH MORNING, HE said a few prayers at a little altar he had created with some crystals, candles, incense and little trinkets that were precious to him. In the middle, he placed a photo of himself as a little boy and one of his mother. As he sat one morning looking at the photo, lit by the flickering light of a candle, he realised that it was as if there were clearly two people inside him: a man and a boy. In the coming days, as the man in him increasingly became okay with the situation and this voice gradually began to establish some authority, the emotional discomfort subsided incrementally. The man's voice within reassured him that a lot had happened recently and that his lover had just gone away for a while to have some time for herself. She had been busy, stressed and tired by her own life's challenges and his behaviour had been extreme. If she didn't realise that she had been a trigger for his emotional purging, it was quite understandable that she would be seriously concerned by his behaviour. It was natural that she would need some time to reflect. If it were meant to be, she would return and if it were not, then she would not.

But the little boy in him was still terrified and traumatised by not knowing whether she would return. For the little boy, this woman was his mother, and it appeared that the scene when his mother had died was being re-enacted. It must have been that as a baby, at some point, he would have been in the warmth, safety, and love of his mother's arms. Then, he would have been given to someone else not knowing that he would never be held by her again. At some point, the tiny baby would have cried for his mother but, of course, she never came. This abandonment trauma that he had experienced at such a tender age was too much for him to process at the time and so it had been stored in his emotional and physical body. Over the years he had revisited this trauma in bite-size chunks of healing, but what he was experiencing now was far more intense than anything he ever had before.

As the days progressed, the man in him began to get the upper hand. He consistently reassured his inner child that everything was fine now; his mother had to leave her body, but she had never really left him at all. His beautiful lover was the siren that had lured him to be shipwrecked on the rocks, but he began to get a sense that the poison that had been blocked and trapped for so long was finally being purged by the sharpness of her decision to leave without knowing whether he would ever see her again. He was undergoing a deep and profound healing.

If he was to continue his exploration of the sacred masculine, he knew that he had to see this ordeal through. There was no-where to run. His sword was in the ground, and he had pledged to face the demon until it was tamed or transformed. As time crawled by, he managed to quiet and soothe the blaming chatter of his despotic inner child and began to feel frequent moments of gratitude for what his lover had set in motion.

On the seventh night, he slept a little more peacefully, and on the eighth day he slept in for the first time since the ordeal had begun. As a result, he did not have time to go for his usual morning walk upon the hills, as he had a long drive to meet with his publisher.

Later that day as he drove back, he enjoyed the familiar view of the hills in the distance. They lay on the horizon; the green and brown ridge like the back of a sleeping dragon. The sight of them always evoked feelings of freedom, peace, and serenity as he made his way home from his travels.

He was tired and soon settled with his cup of tea, his body fused with the sofa and its comfortable cushions. His heart was still aching, though he hardly noticed it anymore; it had become his constant companion. He reassured himself that although she had said she would need a couple of weeks, he was over half way through and surely the second half would pass more quickly and be easier. As he sat in his silent aloneness, sipping some hot, sweet tea, he felt an urge to be up on the ridge. He shifted his body a little and felt the familiar, tired heaviness. He still had hardly managed to eat anything, and he felt frail. But he decided that he would go, reminding himself that there are only two times to go walking: when you feel like it and when you don't feel like it!

As he clambered up the steep incline he centered himself and brought himself into the present by drinking in the beauty that surrounded him with his senses; the buzzard whirling round high above in the grey-blue sky, the delicate whisper of the wind in the green and yellow flecked gorse, the sweet, pungent smell of the earth beneath his bare, trudging feet.

As he walked along, despite his attempts at settling his mind, his thoughts kept returning to wonder if he would ever see her again. He noticed how this thought increased the dull ache in his chest and in that moment a new thought arose. The man in him clearly spoke and said 'If I am meant to be with her, then I shall be and if I am not meant to be with her then so be it. I will be fine. If everything is divinely orchestrated, then so is this.'

In that moment he let go of his attachment to her and, almost immediately, he felt a lightness in his chest that he had not experienced since their drive back up the motorway. His whole body felt less heavy, and he walked, for the first time, with a slight spring in his step. There was a new sensation of pressure in his head, which felt a little odd as he made his way along the path towards his special spot where he planned to rest for a while. He kept reminding himself of his new insight that what would be, would be. Whatever the outcome, he would be fine. An unfamiliar sense of peace took his hand and walked with him.

As he approached his destination, he noticed that someone was already enjoying his favourite spot. The person turned around and, to his complete surprise, it was her.

He staggered back a couple of paces in a moment of fear and disbelief, on once again seeing what, on the surface, appeared to have been the cause of his severe pain.

"What on earth are you doing here?" he stammered.

"I came to meet you," she replied, smiling innocently.

"You said that you would need two weeks. How did you know I would be here?"

"I said," she corrected "that I would need up to two weeks but would be in touch if I gained clarity before."

He vaguely remembered her saying this. He must have chosen to focus on the worst-case scenario.

"And I knew that you would be here because I told them to bring you to me," she grinned, looking very pleased with herself.

"What do you mean?" he asked.

She explained that she had arrived a little while before, as she had wanted some time to be still and quiet before they met. She was going to text him to arrange a time to come to his place. But then she had decided that she would prefer to meet in a more neutral place, so she had asked 'them' to bring him to her. They had responded saying that he would come by at 5:00pm. She had just known that he would.

Looking at her watch, she added "you're actually 2 minutes late."

"Sorry," he said with mock concern "I would have been on time, but I stopped for a pee!"

His flippant remark was an attempt to disguise the strange mixed feelings of shock and delight and fear that he was feeling. He still stood a few meters away and slowly, cautiously, he began to approach her.

Her demeanour suggested to him that she had decided that it was not over between them. A part of him was pleased, another part of him was filled with terror. He had only just minutes before released his attachment to her which had eased his pain and, yet, here she was unexpectedly in front of him. The small hurt voice of pride inside his head wanted to put up some display of uncertainty, maybe suggesting that he was unsure about whether they should resume their relationship, but it didn't stand a chance. He knew he wanted her back. He knew he had already chosen her, and it had always been about whether she would choose him and return to be part of his life.

They spoke a little, and she shared some of what had happened for her in her time alone. It sounded to him as though she had had a wonderful time, for the most part. A bit of him smarted at the discrepancy between his and her experience while they had been apart. By this time, he knew that there was really nothing to forgive and, even if there had been, he would have already forgiven her. Before long they were laid together on her picnic blanket wrapped in each other's arms. He allowed the sensation of relief and release to wash over him while the last remnants of dull heaviness quickly vanished from his body. No more nausea, no more aching heart.

She spoke of how their time together leading up to the Devon break had all been so intense, and the voices and tremors in her body were a little unsettling. Not sleeping well, the pressures of her busy life and some health issues with her mother had all been too much. On top of this, she had a sense that something strange and unknown was stirring deep inside her, too. Sometimes, she hardly recognised herself. The apparent increasing neediness of late and his emotional incontinence had been the last straw and had caused her to withdraw and seek protection by closing and hiding away deep inside herself, like a little girl hiding under the bed covers.

He noticed that she didn't really apologise for her part in what had happened on holiday, but perhaps he didn't need this. Now that she had spoken, he could see things more clearly. He wished that she had shared this with him earlier, but she admitted that she found it incredibly hard to be vulnerable and reveal any weakness. He owned his part in the incident and apologised for getting so emotional and angry. It wasn't an excuse, but to try and help her understand his behaviour, he explained that the scared little boy inside him had played a significant part. He told her a little of what he had been through while she had been away. She looked shocked and was obviously concerned, but at that moment he was very much aware that she could never really know what he had experienced. Anyway, why should she? It was over now, she was back, and she had said that she wanted them to start over afresh. It was all he had ever really wanted.

When they had both said everything that needed to be said they lay together in silence, on their favourite spot, on the hill with the earth and the sky. As his mind and body settled, he began to feel a familiar stirring in his loins. The little boy within him was silent, and the man was fully back.

"Let's go back down the hill to my place," he suggested, adding that it was chilly outside. He was hungry, too.

It wasn't entirely untrue.

When they arrived back at his flat, they ate some simple food that he prepared, and they talked further. He noticed how he wanted her to see things from his perspective and how she was only partially willing or able to do this. It wasn't that he didn't want to take responsibility for his unhelpful behaviour, but he wanted her to see how her lack of communication and honesty had contributed to some extent to his feelings of disconnection, which in turn had triggered his insecurity. In his time alone over the eight days, he realised that he had no right to try and change her. All he could do was change himself, and that meant letting go of his fear of her leaving him. She was not his mother. That had all happened many years ago, and it had no place infiltrating this relationship. She was his lover, his woman, and not his mother. He knew that letting go of attachment to her and reassuring the little boy inside of him were key to making things work between them. Now that things were clearer, he reassured her that things would be different. And he asked her to be as honest with him as possible. She said she would do her best and he never doubted this for one moment.

When it became clear that they had talked enough he joined her on the sofa with a gentle hand on her cheek he turned her head to face his and kissed her slowly on the lips. He moved his head back so that he could look deep into her eyes and wondered how this incredible vision of beauty before him could have been the cause of so much pain. He thanked her silently in his mind, knowing that she had been the catalyst for a powerful trauma release that been so painful. Now it was done and, hopefully, he would never have to go there again. It had been her gift to him.

"Thank you," he said, pulling her to him.

Their mouths met full of hunger and renewed desire. The memory of his last eight days vanished as he took her by the hand and led her to the bedroom. Their reunion was divine. The pain and separation had made them even more hungry for each other, and their sensual coupling reached yet unexperienced heights and depths. Two separate people disappeared, and all that remained was a beautiful fusion of longing, desire, and pleasure; the ultimate sacred, primal dance of man and woman.

By the time their naked bodies were asleep under the soft coolness of the bedcovers it was as if their eight days apart had never happened.

CHAPTER 10

After the intense emotional purging, he was sure that the majority of trauma trapped in his body was transformed. As a result, things would begin to be easier between them. After all, she had decided to come back, and now there was so much more awareness around why he had been so emotionally triggered. They could surely work with any remnants of his past that might reappear and create challenges between them. It was so ironic that her behaviour was the perfect catalyst to elicit his mother bereavement trauma, but now that he had identified the wounded little boy inside him, he was mindful of any old patterns creeping back in. They had both agreed to be more open and honest, and he felt sure that this was the key ingredient to ensuring that things would stay easy and sweet.

By way of an apology for his emotional behaviour, and in an attempt to put the whole unpleasant incident behind them, he decided to book another weekend away. They needed a positive experience of going away together to cancel out the last one. She had shared with him how she was concerned that he did not share her passion for culture and the arts. He did his best to reassure her that this needn't be a big deal, as he was willing to learn more about this side of her life. They didn't have to share all the same interests. It was a good time to put his money where his mouth was, and he knew that the weekend would need to include a cultural element to it. He thought about asking her son for some clues as to where to take her, but in the end, he decided to just wait a while and see if an idea presented itself.

As he was driving home from a work appointment one evening, a program came on the radio about an art gallery in Yorkshire. He made a mental note of it and decided to do some research when he got home. It turned out that it was not too far away, and it looked like just the sort of thing that she would enjoy. In addition, it was situated very near to some areas of outstanding natural beauty so they could enjoy their love of walking, too. He was ready to be exposed to more culture, partly because he knew it would be enriching for him, as new experiences are nearly always a good idea, and partly because he knew how important it was to her.

They found a date in the diary when they were both able to take time off work. He didn't tell her where they were going but had to concede to her repeated requests to give some indication of what sort of clothes she needed to pack. He wasn't good at keeping secrets, but he made up his mind that he would not tell her where they were going until they set off on the appointed day.

He booked a lovely little cottage for them in rural Yorkshire and was feeling very pleased with himself. All he had to do was keep his mouth shut and not give in to her girlish requests for clues as to where they were going.

THE DAYS ROLLED by with work commitments and meetings with friends and the everyday tasks that needed to be done to keep on top of the demands of twenty-first century life. Text and Messenger messages punctuated the gentle undulations of his life, and occasionally they would video call and have conversations, too. But he was increasingly aware that he still wanted more communication with her than he was having. He could call her, and she said that she was happy to talk more between weekends, but she rarely initiated calls to him. The man in him knew that this was perfectly natural for her to not call. It was him who wanted more communication; after all, he was the one who had more free time, and she was the one who was always busy. However, the little boy in him still felt needy at times and wanted to hear the reassurance of her voice and confirmation that all was well between them. He knew this was totally irrational and he reassured the little boy in his head as much as possible.

Although things were much less intense than they had been, he became progressively aware that his old wound was not yet fully healed. He was going to have to be very vigilant and mindful to prevent his fear from sabotaging his chances of growing a strong connection with this beautiful woman under whose spell he had so willingly fallen. His main adversary was his constant awareness of how connected or unconnected he felt with her and, rather than enjoying the fullness of their time together, his mind kept looking at things from a glass half empty perspective. The most worrying thought that kept recurring was that she had not taken any responsibility for the drama that had happened in Devon. He knew that his insecurity arose when there was a lack of connection between them. He had clearly felt this disconnect between them, and he guessed that she had withdrawn due to her fear of revealing more darkness from her past. Secrets always create a distance, and his sensitive, empathic nature was highly aware of this. Perhaps she didn't believe that he could feel when there was a lack of connection between them. Maybe she genuinely thought that secrets did not create a distance. It was possible that she really did feel that he had just massively overreacted. In some ways he had, but he began to notice more and more that he was treading on eggshells in relation to what he said and their communication in general. In truth, his challenge was to accept her just as she was and to focus on the only thing that he had any semblance of control over, himself.

To make matters worse, she seemed especially emotional and touchy of late, so he tried his best not to say things that she might find upsetting for fear that she would withdraw and stonewall him. But this meant that he wasn't always speaking his truth. He wondered whether he was capable of keeping his fearful emotions at bay and his mouth shut.

Every couple of weeks he spent time with his mentor, where the bulk of their conversations were about the latest challenges in his romantic relationship. He expressed his frustrations and fear, and the terrifyingly strong emotions that he felt. His mentor would listen attentively, periodically asking probing questions to elicit a deeper understanding. Other times, he would offer advice. On leaving the sessions he always felt better and clearer, but before too long his mind would begin whispering unhelpful thoughts. He found it hard to discern what was actually happening and what was just a projection of his own fears and insecurities.

Apart from the wonderful sexual chemistry and the love of nature that they shared, the other powerful connecting factor that they had in common was their love, practise and exploration of spirituality. Since they had met, unusual happenings were becoming more frequent for both. There was strong catalytic energy that was created in their union.

One evening, as they sat in candlelight at his flat, she asked him to fetch the hairbrush so that she could comb his hair. He loved having his hair brushed, and he was soon sat on the floor with his back leaning against the sofa. She began to gently run the brush through his long thick hair. When she had finished, they remained where they were sat and soaked up the gentle energy that was almost tangible in the room. In the quiet and serene stillness of the moment, she began to tremble and shake quite considerably.

"Can you feel her?" she asked. "your mother is here."

He could feel a deep stillness inside him but was unaware of any presence that he could associate with a person.

"No, I can't," he replied. For some reason, he began to cry.

A small gasp escaped from her, but he could see that she was okay, although she had a faraway look in her eyes. He just sat where he was and allowed the tears to fall, and the soft energy seemed to swirl around him. After a little while, she stopped trembling completely and sank a little deeper into the sofa.

"Are you okay?" he asked.

"Yes," she replied. "I am just fine, but oh my god, could you feel the love? There was so much love in the room; you are so loved. Couldn't you feel it?"

He confessed that he could not, though the tears were still not dry on his face. Something had clearly happened, and the deep stillness that had arisen for both was carried into the bedroom a little later where it permeated their soft, gentle lovemaking.

Another time, they were her at her place, talking quite casually in the kitchen. The mood was light and playful, and he teased her by saying,

"Well, you should know better; after all, being a year older than me, you are the eldest!"

Suddenly, she let out a loud shriek. She reached out her hand to him, and he held her arm to steady her.

"What's wrong?" he asked, concerned.

"Something's happening," she said.

The faraway look had appeared in her eyes again. He stood beside her while she gazed into the distance for a minute or two until she began to return as if re-emerging from a trance. She appeared a little distressed, and he instinctively led her outside where she could feel the fresh air on her face and her bare feet on the grass.

He brought her some water, which she sipped slowly as she returned to her usual self. She apologised for her behaviour as she seemed to be feeling a little embarrassed, but he reassured her that it was all fine. He rather liked what he called the 'magic' that seemed to be a regular part of their journey together.

When she was feeling more grounded, she explained to him that she had seen a vision of herself from a past time wearing ceremonial clothes. In the vision, she was a leader of some sort, and behind her, there were many women of different generations who she felt an amazing sense of connection and belonging to. She stood with her arms outstretched and a staff in her hand as if she was saying some important words.

She was a little disturbed by what had happened, and he did his best to reassure her that she would understand what she had seen more clearly.

It seemed to have been triggered by him saying 'you are the eldest.' Perhaps she was a very ancient soul, and her vision was something to do with this. They would probably never know for sure, but he didn't mind. He liked the otherworldly dimension to his woman. It only added to the allure and strong attraction that he felt for her and the sense that they were meant to be together. The unusual occurrences became just another part of their adventure.

HE WAS ON his way to her cottage to whisk her away on their surprise adventure weekend. He was optimistic that all would be well. When she opened the door, he was met with her gleaming smile, pretty eyes and glowing presence; any slight concerns in the back of his mind vanished immediately. Most of the time when he was with her everything felt just fine. He wondered how he could let his mind come up with so many problems and get so antsy in the spaces between their togetherness.

They were soon in his car speeding up the M42, and he smiled inwardly at the thought of three whole days together. More connection and conversation and good fun were bound to be what was needed, he thought, and light-hearted conversation flowed easily between them as they headed North.

She always seemed to have so much to say, and he enjoyed listening to her talking about this and that. He remembered her saying that often she was quiet and reserved, so he took her chattiness as a sign that she was comfortable with him. This was what he wanted more than anything. He knew that while his fear radar was hyper-vigilant, looking for reasons why he should not open his heart fully, the same was probably going on for her. But, for now, they were together, and as the miles brought them closer to their weekend's cosy home, he settled into the ebb and flow of conversation while the countryside gradually merged into the soft hills and valleys of South Yorkshire.

They arrived in the late afternoon but were too early to check in. They decided to go for a walk to get a feel for the local countryside and stretch their legs.

They soon found themselves following a small footpath around the edge of a village. They walked holding hands, enjoying the fresh air and absorbing the vista. In front of them was a green expanse of fields, divided by grey drystone walls that were dotted with little scruffy copses here and there. The air was cool at first, but as they walked the clouds dispersed to reveal a deep blue sky and the sun warmed them. He took his shirt off and carried it in his hand.

They stopped for a while at an old wooden five bar gate and took in the beauty of the landscape around them. After a while, he jumped down and stood in front of her where she sat on the gate and patted the base of his back.

"Jump on," he said. "It's time for a piggyback ride."

She offered a weak protest, suggesting that she would be too heavy, but he would have none of it.

"Come on, you are going for a ride," he insisted.

Gingerly, and a little clumsily, she lowered herself onto him with her hands clasped together around his neck, laughing nervously. He held her legs and hitched her up a little before setting off at a gentle canter around the field. She whooped and shrieked with delight while he whinnied and neighed to accompany his improvised horse impersonation. Before too long he lowered her gently to the ground and fell to the floor laughing and gasping for air to oxygenate the muscles in his tired legs. She fell down beside him, and they lay together in the lush green grass. Anchored by the earth beneath them, they gazed up at the sky, watching the grey and white clouds morphing and drifting by.

They cuddled and kissed a little, and he felt so alive. He was grateful for every detail of his rich and varied life, that in some way had led him to be in the here and now, sharing this beautiful moment with her.

Eventually, they made their way back to the car, only to find that they had completely lost track of time. There were four missed calls on his mobile phone as the owners of their booked accommodation had been waiting for them. He was mortified, as he really disliked letting people down. She did her best to reassure him that it wasn't a big deal while they drove the short distance back down to the village.

Understandably, the owner of the cottage was rather curt; she had been waiting for over an hour and had just been about to give up on them and drive away. They were given a quick tour and instructions about where to leave the key on their departure, and then they were alone again.

They quickly unpacked and set about heating up the food that she had prepared the previous day. She was a good cook, and the stew with crusty brown bread was tasty and wholesome. Its nourishing warmth matched the warm ambiance of the little cottage, and soon they were snuggled on the sofa together watching a DVD from the collection on the shelf.

They managed to loosely focus on the movie for about an hour before the gentle caresses and closeness of their bodies overpowered them. Pretty soon his trousers and shorts were off, and he lay on his back on the sofa with her sat up on top of him. There had been no time to remove her bra and her belly gyrated while her hips rhythmically pulsed erotically as she moved expertly to ensure that she could feel the maximum amount of contact and stimulation of him inside her. She was a different creature when she was on top, with him inside. Her blonde hair was tossed back, and her eyes were closed; she rode him confidently, grinning with pleasure while running her tongue seductively around her moist, pink lips. He drank in the blissful view and the delicious sensations in his loins intensified as she adjusted herself so that she was laid on top of him in her favourite position; soon, it would bring her to climax. Her pleasure was so completely his, and he fondled her breasts and kissed and licked her neck as she moaned louder and louder as the ecstasy of orgasm engulfed her. He held her tenderly, and when her breathing had settled a little, he gently slid himself from under her. He offered her his hand, and she took it, and he led her up the small crooked stairs to the bedroom. He pulled back the bedcovers so that she could collapse onto her back on the cool, white, cotton sheets.

"Spread your legs for me, honey," he commanded softly.

She gave him a quizzical look, but she did as she was asked and in no time at all he was on her and in her, holding her tightly. He pulsed slowly and fully into her with a gentle, sure rhythm and then, gradually, he moved faster and faster. When it seemed that her cries and limp, exhausted form could take no more, he would ease off and slow down again. Sometimes, he remained motionless inside her while their eyes locked, searching deep into each other. In the stillness, something magical would happen in the soft energy that engulfed him. Then, he would move to the beat of a deep primal drum once again, strong and loud in his chest. The vision of her beauty added its magic to their sensual harmony, and soon he lay beside her as his gift to her oozed gently onto the sheets between her soft, warm thighs.

AFTER EATING A hasty breakfast, they left for the art gallery. He had never been to an art gallery before and was curious as to how he would find the experience. He was perhaps too conscious of the fact that she would be noting how he responded to this cultural outing because culture was so important to her. He always wore his heart on his sleeve, and he knew that if he were bored, he would not be able to hide it. He hoped it wouldn't come to that and, instead, that he would enjoy himself. He did his best to dispel any nagging thoughts of how he was just trying to please her. Though, to some extent, he was really trying to win her over and prove to her that they were compatible.

They arrived at the gallery and wandered around, taking in the exhibits. Sometimes they were together and sometimes apart, although he liked to be able to see her and always made sure that he knew which room she was in. He tried to really immerse himself in the paintings, but he found most of them uninteresting. A few exhibits did arouse his curiosity, and he let his imagination ponder the story behind the painting. She shared with him the different feelings that different paintings evoked for her, but he was aware that he felt very little stir within. He found the place stuffy and very heady. The energy seemed to be very intense, almost close and oppressive as though a thunderstorm needed to happen. So, he just ambled around and brought his attention back to the present. He reminded himself that this was another unique experience that had its place in the rich myriad of experiences that made up his life and the adventure of being human. Mostly, he was just glad to be with her, and he was secretly proud that he had organised the trip to help show her how important she was to him. He could see that she was pleased to be there, and this was the best thing about it all.

After a couple of hours, she was culturally satiated. After buying herself a little souvenir, they left. They made their way back to the parked car and headed South in the direction of home. As he drove, she asked him whether he had enjoyed the art gallery and he told her that he had. He focused on the positive elements of his experience and deliberately omitted some details. He felt that his response was important, that she was interested to see whether there was any possibility of him growing to accompany her passion for art galleries and such. He was curious to know what her assessment was but reminded himself that the secret of success in a relationship was for them both to accept each other as they were. There was nothing he could do about it if she were not willing to accept him as he was.

After driving for a while, they decided to stop for a drink. They were in no hurry to get home and, even though they both had work in the morning, they wanted to make their little adventure last as long as possible.

In a small Yorkshire village, they found a scruffy little pub that was occupied by some farmers and elderly local gentlemen. It had a peculiar mismatched and uncoordinated style to the old, musty decor and they felt very out of place and conspicuous as they waited to be served at the bar. Seated with drinks and crisps, they giggled quietly and whispered to each other at the unusual décor of the place. He shuffled up closer to her on the musty old bench and put his arm around her waist, squeezing her to him.

Before long, they were strolling hand in hand around the village. They chanced upon a lovely little cobbled street, lined with old cottages with roses and climbing plants growing up trellises attached to the walls. It created an idyllic backdrop for the final moments of their break. He asked her to pause so that he could take her photo and she agreed this time, though she stood looking slightly uncomfortable in the presence of the camera. It sometimes seemed that it was as if she wanted and needed to be seen, yet at the same time, she desperately did not want to be seen. Taking her photo always made him aware of this contradiction, and he sighed inwardly.

He showed her the photos on his mobile, and she scrolled through quickly, letting him know which one she disliked the least. He thought she looked stunning in all of them, framed as she was by the rustic scene of old stone, wooden window frames and iron hinged doors with various coloured flowers smiling sweetly. Nevertheless, he deleted them all except for the one which she had chosen.

By the time they neared her home, it was getting late, and they stopped at a local Indian restaurant for dinner. They were tired, and though he held her hand and looked into her lovely eyes adoringly, he was aware that there was a hint of anxiety and fear lurking in the shadows. The trip away had been a success, they had a lovely time, though his mind had found a new tool to torment him and it goaded him with the idea that his lack of culture would be a reason for her to leave him.

THEY MADE LOVE in the morning before they were even fully awake. Morning sex felt different to night time sex. There was something untidier and more natural and juicy about it. He loved having her without her make-up and her hair ungroomed and wild; there was the sweet smell of perspiration and sleep, and the whole thing felt a little raw and primal! After, as he lay breathing heavily beside her, he gazed in awe at her. He noted how she seemed to wear so many different faces; there were so many different aspects of her, and he was bewitched by all of them.

"As you lay there, darling, you look so plain."

She winced, and he knew immediately that he had said something wrong.

"Plain?" she said with an air of disbelief. She turned her back on him.

He tried his best to explain himself, but it was clear that somehow, she had been offended by his comment.

"But, darling, you know how beautiful I find you. It's just another facet of your beauty; an innocent, girlish beauty. It may be that plain is not the right word. I didn't mean to upset you."

He squirmed and writhed inside with discomfort, feeling a sense of panic and fear rising in him. With her back to him he had felt her close down, lock him out.

He stroked her hair and kissed her naked back apologetically. He wished that he could redeem himself by finding a different word to describe the beauty that he had noted in her angelic face.

After a little while, she turned over and faced him.

"Do you mean natural?" she asked with a softer expression on her face.

"Yes," he said quickly. "Yes, that is a better word. That is what I meant."

She agreed that it was a better word. It seemed that she sometimes knew that she was oversensitive and emotional and the fact that she had turned to face him again so quickly made him feel that she was trying her best to be less emotional and touchy. As he held and stroked her, she quickly re-emerged from her icy fortress, and they snuggled under the warmth of the covers. They lay and chatted together about the highlights of the weekend, and she thanked him earnestly for the care and consideration that he had taken in planning and organising the trip. He felt a warm glow, yet he also knew that before long, time would demand that he leave her. They would soon throw the bed covers back, shower and dress, say goodbye and embark on their separate day's commitments again. It never seemed as if there was enough time. He always wanted more of her. So, when she suddenly suggested that they go abroad together, somewhere in Europe where the heat of the sun was guaranteed, he was delighted!

They agreed on a week in Southern Portugal. The dates were quickly agreed and recorded in diaries. While he showered and dressed, she began to research places to stay on her phone. He kissed her tenderly on her soft lips where she lay under the covers, inhaled one last waft of her sweet morning fragrance, and left hurriedly for his first meeting of the day.

CHAPTER 11

In between their time together, he missed her. He just always felt as if he was waiting. Sometimes, when he was feeling brave, he would tell her in his messages. She would often reply saying that she too missed him, but it didn't always help. He could tell that she was cooler about the time they spent apart and again his mischievous mind would sow seeds of doubt and fear. He would do his best to reassure himself that all was well, that it was okay to miss her so intensely. If she said that she missed him, too, then that was good enough. Still, he had a growing sense that it was almost impossible to discern between the feelings of fear and love. To what extent did he love her and to what extent was he just fearful of losing her? Was this real love or was it just a needy longing because he felt incomplete in himself? Was it that he really wanted to be with her or was it just that the time without her made him realise how little he wanted to be with himself?

These thoughts tormented him, only finding solace when he remembered the words 'Bring him home.'

He knew that she was facilitating some deep healing within him. Perhaps they would grow old together. Perhaps she was just meant to be with him long enough to finally do the last healing of an old wound that he had been carrying for too long. Either way, what would be, would be. His task was just to remain as present as possible and not get lost in fear. She was in his life now, and that was a blessing.

He sometimes pondered on her own healing process. She was very aware that she had issues about communication, vulnerability and being open, but it sometimes seemed that she wasn't conscious of the full extent of this. It was as if in some ways they were at different ends of the spectrum. Sometimes he knew that he wanted to communicate and share too much and that he needed to find ways of finding resolution with himself; that everything did not have to be discussed for the air to be cleared. And for her, she knew that she needed to be less autonomous at times and speak more freely and share what she was thinking. It was obvious that life had brought them together so that they could learn from each other and heal.

It had become clear to him recently that much of our journey to wholeness and peace is dependent on the work we do to honour and heal the divine twin flame union of masculine and feminine within. When the marriage of our masculine and feminine divinity is strong, clear and conscious, we know that our childhood wounds have become scars. This, in turn, means that we are free to engage in relationships, romantic or otherwise, that are not seen through the lens of the wounded inner child but from a clear and clean adult presence. He intensely desired a connection with her that was free from co-dependency.

SHE CONTINUED TO work hard in her café, although staffing issues seemed to be a constant challenge that meant she often had to do two people's work. She found great satisfaction in the positive feedback from customers, though she often spoke of how she wished that she could do more to help people less fortunate than herself. He did his best to reassure her that she was making a positive contribution to the lives of everyone who came to her café. They may have thought that they had just stopped by for a drink and a bite to eat but were probably also drawn by the sweet energy of the place that was assured of having a positive effect on their well-being. It's not so much about what you do, as how you do what you do, that often is the most important factor in contribution and service.

She had finally finished her college course, and he was hopeful that they might start to see each other in the middle of the week. Or, at the very least, have a few more phone conversations. But this never really happened. She was always tired, and a steady flow of family dramas sapped any extra energy and time that she might have gained by completing her studies.

His career continued to amble along, and he was aware that he wasn't really breaking any new ground. The promotion of his previous books became a little tedious and work on his current project was slow, to say the least. He wrote for a few online magazines regularly and was sometimes interviewed on various shows, but he still felt like a mediocre wannabe author. He was aware that so much of his creative energy was going into his romantic relationship. When things were clear and close between them, he was overawed by the intensity of the delicious emotions that he felt. These were the times when he wrote. He couldn't help himself it was as if his words were always and only for her. At times he just had to write, as if the richness and intensity of the feeling needed some escape, and so they overflowed onto the page. It was too much to contain within his body.

How could walking hand in hand through a farmers' market be such an intimate experience? How could sharing food together in a crowded restaurant be so divine? How could a trip to the cinema be so much fun?

He only really wanted to write for her, and so he did. He wrote poems and emails and messages and continued to write handwritten letters, which he posted to her in the old-fashioned way. He would always seal them with the melted wax and his Celtic triple spiral stamp. She was his muse, but the fruits of his creativity, the words that she evoked from his heart, were too personal to share with the world.

OFTEN, OUR MOST significant inspirations are unexpected. Sometimes, they begin with a bucket of apples.

Each morning he began his day with a freshly pressed juice, which included apples that he had been gifted from his friend's orchard. On this particular morning when he opened the back door, in addition to the apples, in the bucket was also a mouse. It had climbed in but was unable to get back out. After taking a quick photo of the little creature, he bent down and tilted the bucket so that the little prisoner could escape to freedom.

After his juice, he sat at his desk and decided to share the photo on his blog. He wrote a short explanation of the photograph, and a short story emerged. He imagined how the mouse had come to be there and what had happened after he was freed from the bucket. Of course, with all his writings, he wanted to send them to his muse, and so he emailed the little story over.

That evening when they spoke on the telephone, she was effusive in her delight at the story. He was a little taken aback, as the story had just tumbled out onto the page by itself, he didn't really think that it was anything special. But she was adamant that it would make a beautiful children's story and that he should send it to some potential publishers.

She was always so encouraging about his writing. Being a published author, one might have expected him to be totally confident and aware of his ability to write well. Instead, there was often a nagging fear at the back of his mind that the success to date was just a fluke and that he would never be able to write anything of value again. Her love and appreciation for the words he wrote helped him to believe in himself and this latest enthusiasm for the short mouse story was most welcome. Being such a lover of books, she was well read, and he trusted her judgment, so he polished the story a little and did some research online. By the end of the day, the story had been emailed to a handful of publishers. All he could do was to see if anyone else concurred with her appreciation of his writing.

To his surprise, within a couple of weeks, a letter arrived from a reputable publisher, along with a contract. He immediately called her, and she screamed and cried out in delight on the other end of the phone.

"I told you so," she taunted. "I told you that you are an extremely talented writer. Now perhaps you will believe me!"

She was right, of course. Right that it was time for him to really start believing in himself and stop playing small. He was so grateful for her encouragement, and he knew that this was another of the many gifts that she brought into his life. He looked at his new good fortune in the light of his relationship, reasoning that this new success as an author might increase his self-worth. Conceivably, it would make him less needy, which could only benefit their relationship. This new addition to his career as a children's author, he owed to her. He would not have put his story forward if it hadn't been for her effusive insistence.

And yet, despite his renewed self-belief and his deepened gratitude to her, the time between their meetings was still challenging for him. The fear that he would lose her lingered around the periphery of his awareness. Sometimes, when they were together, he would say something, and she would respond with a look. No words were uttered, but he thought he detected a hint of disapproval in her glance. When he would ask her to share her thoughts, she would decline and just smile sweetly. He didn't want to push her for fear of rocking the boat and spoiling their precious time together. So, the moment would pass and, like a neglected cupboard where all the things are kept that we should throw away but don't, his mind got more and more cluttered. Possible bits of evidence constantly tried to sabotage their togetherness.

He did his best to let go of his concerns, though he was worried that perhaps she was not committed to staying with him or building a life together. After all, they had only known each other for about six months; he really needed to just chill out a bit!

He worked hard to let go of the feeling that she was collecting an anthology of reasons why they should not be together. Was it that these thoughts created a feeling of anxiety inside him or was that feeling always there, and he was making up reasons to attach the feelings to? Was he making it all up? He knew that trying to work his mind out with his mind was an impossible task, but what could he do? If he spoke to her of his concerns, she would often get defensive and emotionally withdraw from him, which was what he most feared. Then he would find it difficult not to express his frustration and anger at her response, but if he spoke to her of his frustration, his unwelcome energy would cause her to withdraw further. He knew that she struggled with conflict; even if he raised his voice a little, she would threaten to end the conversation or complain that she was feeling tired and didn't want to talk anymore. From her perspective, they had been talking for long enough. From his perspective, they had only just got started. He firmly believed that when things seemed most difficult that meant, they could be on the point of a breakthrough. After a storm, the air always feels clearer, but because of her fear of conflict, it seldom felt as though the storm had been able to do its work. For him, the air rarely seemed totally clear.

So, for the most part, he resigned himself to his fate. He hoped that his awareness and mindfulness would be enough to prevent him from reacting and that his fearful mind would not get the better of him. If only they could be together more, it would be easier. It was always in the spaces between their meetings that his mind had the most power to create unhelpful stories that he found it hard not to get lost in.

He feared that he had been giving too much thought to the relationship, especially when they were not together. He often felt that she did not give their relationship sufficient thought, but maybe she was just much busier than him. Did he simply have more time and energy to contemplate their connection? What would be enough for him? It was possible that there would always be a feeling that he wanted more, that however much she gave would never be enough. He knew that he needed to be more complete unto himself, yet he found it so hard to not lose his sense of self in the story of their togetherness. He found the fine line of discernment between contacting her enough so that she knew how much he cared about her and not contacting her too much to not appear needy, almost impossible. It all became like a dance routine which he didn't really know the steps and the music was getting faster and faster.

BY THE TIME their holiday in Portugal had arrived, the energy between them was a little strained, to say the least. He knew it was, but he chose to ignore it because at last, they were going to have a whole seven days together. The pool at the beautiful villa they had booked would be warm, and the sand on the beach would be white and dazzling under the bright heat of the golden sun. The cleansing salt water of the ocean would wash away any fears, and they could relax and make love and eat good food.

They arrived late at night, and their hire car pulled up outside the villa to the sound of crickets and the gentle warmth of the fragrant night air. They fumbled with the key in the door and tumbled into the bedroom with suitcases in tow. She sat down on the bed with a sigh of relief, but it collapsed under her in an undignified thud. Their initial laughter soon turned to annoyance. They moved to the other bedroom where he hurriedly pushed the two beds together. They carefully got into bed, this time without event, and she was soon asleep while he lay listening to the night sounds. In the silence, he allowed his thoughts to meander. It always seemed a cruel joke to him, how men generally need to make love to feel close, while women need to feel close to make love. He looked across at the back of her beneath the sheet and, in her defense, he reminded himself that if you are completely exhausted, then that is going to be a significant factor, too!

Much to his delight, she woke up with morning sex on her mind, too. Her body yielded to his touch while their mouths and tongues enjoyed each other.

The warmth of the Portuguese air meant that there was no need for bed covers, and he enjoyed this new lovers' freedom. Her cries of delight and passion soon echoed gently in the emptiness of the room. She writhed naked beneath him her legs pinned open by his thighs while his fingers enjoyed her hot, slippery wetness.

It didn't matter what was going on between them when they made love the world disappeared. There was only the delicious moment of connection, desire, and passion; the carnal delight of naked flesh upon naked flesh and the longing to give and receive pleasure. How religions had ever come up with the ridiculous notion that the delight of consensual lovemaking was a sin was beyond him. Her hips twitched and writhed under his expert attention. With her right hand, she took hold of his lower back and pulled him to her. With her left, she pulled at his wrist, a request to remove his fingers; she wanted him inside her.

He made her wait a few more moments before yielding to the demands of her hands and then gave her what she wanted. He always loved the sound she made as he entered her for the first time, the gentle moan of exquisite pleasure at finally having that which she had so impatiently been waiting for. He would postpone the moment of penetration as long as possible, knowing that it could be the beginning of the end, as he was not always controlled enough to resist ejaculation.

Although he allowed his energy and the power and frequency of his plunges to ebb and flow to some extent, the point of no return came unexpectedly, and the noise, the smell, the feel, the taste, the sight of her was all too much. He had no choice but to surrender any restraint he had and allow his body to do as it wished. The energy inevitably rose higher and higher, and he drove himself harder and harder inside her while his hands and wrists held her luscious buttocks in his firm grip. She climaxed first, and her body convulsed as wave after wave of energy coursed through her until he, driven even wilder by her cries of ecstasy, continued until his sacred fire was released inside her and it was his turn to groan and cry out with pleasure.

They lay side by side, panting and perspiring, while the distant sound of cars occasionally punctuated the still, warm silence. It was always like this. The perfect space they inhabited after making love was so sacred.

As THE WORLD began to return, she opened the shutters and looked out. To their dismay there was no blue sky and no sun to be seen, only thick grey clouds filled the sky. She checked the weather app on her phone, and it confirmed that the day would be cloudy with occasional showers. What made things worse was that the next five-day forecast threatened the same dismal weather, which was unheard of in The Algarve at this time of year. He did his best to reassure her as she protested disconsolately that this would be her only foreign holiday of the year; she had wanted so much to enjoy some sunshine. On top of this, she noticed three bites on her legs which were already becoming itchy and uncomfortable. Although she had been taking antihistamine tablets prior to leaving, they seemed to be having little effect. She was prone to strong reactions from mosquitos and was worried that they would get even worse.

After showering they made sure that she was covered in insect repellent and that the insect mosquito plugins were all in working order. But it was clear that she was not in a good mood; tired, bitten and a grim weather forecast was not the start to the holiday that they had wished for.

He did his best to take care of her and reassure her that weather forecasts weren't always right while he struggled with his own feelings. In her unhappiness, she seemed further away from him. He felt an increase in the general sense of disconnection that he had been aware of over recent weeks and this pressed his own buttons. They had a whole week together to look forward to, and the weather wasn't a big deal for him, but, for some reason, he felt uneasy. His infuriating mind insisted on bringing up every possible piece of evidence to convince him that she would never love him. Like a movie on repeat, he remembered her reaction when he had told her how he loved her. He wanted to confess everything he felt to her. He wanted to confess his weakness and insecurity and that, although they had only made love so beautifully a few hours earlier, it seemed as if she was a million miles away from him. He wanted so much for it to be how it had been when they first met. He wanted to talk about everything; instead, they went shopping at the supermarket.

Later in the afternoon they swam in the pool and relaxed on the sun loungers with books. There was no sun, but it was warm, and at least there wasn't any rain yet. But, like the black clouds above, the black fearful clouds within him were gathering, too. She remained immersed in her book and was dismissive of any attempts he made for them to converse. She probably just needed space and time to unwind and get over her disappointment at the weather. Her bites, now growing larger, itchier and hotter, were not helping matters.

And then the storm broke; not in the sky above them, but in the villa. An insensitive comment that he made was all that it took to set light to the dry and parched tinder box. She snapped at him like a preying-mantis that had been waiting to pounce. He did his best to defend himself and in so doing raised his voice. It was an attempt to make her see how she was overreacting, even though he was overreacting himself. She walked away, saying that she didn't want to talk about it, and that was it; like a red rag to a bull, her reluctance to discuss the issue and clear the air inflamed his anger. He shouted and berated her while she closed down, and he saw the icy shutters slide into place around her. He was alone with his fear again.

He knew he had to give her some space and that he had probably already said too much, yet he was furious inside. He was furious with himself for not being calmer, furious with her for not seeing how she was partly responsible for their falling out, furious at the weather and the mosquitos and everything.

He rolled a cigarette and smoked it by the pool, but it tasted horrible and did nothing to take the edge off the intensity of emotion that he was feeling. There was nothing that he could do. He wanted to leave, he wanted to take the car and drive, but there was nowhere that he wanted to be in this foreign land. He hated the fact that she was only a dozen meters away from him in the bedroom, though she might as well have been on another planet.

After a few hours, she came out of her room and sat reading on the sofa as if nothing had happened. There was no attempt at reconciliation, and this angered him, too. How could she switch her emotions off in that way? How was she able to focus on reading while inside him the storm still raged?

After what seemed like an eternity, and much pacing around, calmness returned, and a peace began to descend again. He went to her and tried to make amends, but pretty soon they were arguing again, and this time she shouted, too, and threw her food at him. It was a feeble attempt at violence, and he couldn't help but laugh, which didn't go down too well since she was pretty worked up, too.

The day dragged on, and they ate some food together that he had prepared in an awkward semi-silence. Eventually, it was time for bed, and he prayed that sleep would soon come so that he could have an end to the terrible start to their much looked forward to holiday.

It was not to be. He lay awake next to her while she slept and again, he was perplexed and enraged that she should be able to sleep while he suffered his emotional turmoil alone. He knew he was massively overreacting. He knew that this wasn't just about what she or he had said or done, it was an accumulation of past events, both recent and long gone. It was as if he was ensnared on a short leash and his mind yanked him this way and that with vicious thoughts, which only increased the fear and emotion that he felt in his body.

He shouldn't have done it, but he did. He woke her from her sleep and again tried to get her to see his point of view in some lame attempt to find closeness and connection. He apologised half-heartedly, but his apology was paper thin, and she knew it. He was lost; he didn't know what was right and what was wrong anymore. He tried in vain to find a way out of the emotional maze that he was lost in. She was in no mood to help him, though, wanting only for him to let her sleep.

He had no choice but to feel what he was feeling, and he lay listening to her breath as she quickly returned to the sanctuary of sleep. While he tossed and turned, the emotion in his exhausted body settled and his mind conceded to his desperate pleas to allow him to rest and sleep, too.

HE APOLOGISED FOR his behaviour again in the morning and, as the hours passed, the distance between them diminished. A kind word here and a comment there and the storm became a distant memory. There was no real resolution or understanding as to what was at the root of the argument, as usual. However, she made it clear that they were not going to talk about it, that it was time to move on. They were on holiday, and even though the weather was still alarmingly unseasonal, they had to make the best of it. They decided to jump in the car and go see some caves, that were not too far away.

The rest of the holiday improved more quickly than the weather. They bought an umbrella and drove the coast road both north and south, visiting quaint Portuguese towns, perusing the shops and enjoying the rich, tasty culinary delights of the local restaurants.

It was refreshing to be away from the push and pull of appointments and deadlines and diaries and mobile phones. They agreed to turn their phones off, only putting them on in the evening to check for any important messages from family or work. How liberating to just make the basic decisions like where, what, and when to eat. To never have to rush, to lounge about and read or go for a walk or drive, to be able to make love whenever the urge arose, which it did quite regularly.

They made love in the pool; her legs wrapped around him as he stood firmly against the wall. They made love on the balcony, where she knelt and enjoyed him in her lascivious mouth while he ran his fingers roughly through her untidy hair. And they made love in the lounge until she screamed so loudly with delight that they closed the patio doors for fear that the distant neighbours might hear and be alarmed.

Although the sky was still grey much of the time, they enjoyed the freedom of just wearing swimwear or sarongs. Enjoying her semi-nakedness as they hung out at the villa was an extra source of pleasure for him. At times, he would surprise her by pulling her to him and kissing her, already aroused by the passing movement of her hips and curves beneath her thin, pink cotton sarong. She never resisted, and her body soon met him in his state of arousal as they satiated their seemingly unending desire for one another.

The last three days of the holiday brought the blessing of some sunshine, and they made the most of the time that remained on the beach. The sand was white and contrasted with the clear blue sea that reflected the refreshingly new blue of the wide sky.

He was not a fan of clothes when the climate was conducive to nakedness. It seemed crazy to him that one should be encumbered by garments when the temperature was warm because there was little more beautiful than the caress of the wind upon naked flesh, or the kiss of the sun. Uncomfortable, soggy, wet swimming trunks perplexed him. He had spent time on nudist beaches, but she had not. They spoke about this, and he encouraged her to remove her bikini top if she wanted to, as there were other topless women on the beach. She didn't respond, but he could see she was thinking about it. When he returned from a short walk, he found her topless on her back. She looked relaxed and beautiful, and he wondered again how he could be so lucky as to be sharing his life with such an attractive woman. While she snoozed, he stole a few photos of her. He would confess his crime later!

The mood between them remained good. There were no more storms, but the unease in the periphery of his awareness was constant, apart from brief interludes when they made love. Most of the time he allowed her to make the choices and decisions, such as where and when to eat, because she seemed happy to be in control, but sometimes she would get frustrated when he would say "I don't mind," in response to her questions.

He did his best to find a balance between being assertive, decisive and masculine, and when to allow her to take the lead, but it was not always clear what was required of him. The truth was that they were both so used to being alone and not having to consider another all the time that they were still finding their way. Perhaps there will always be challenges when mature people come together in a romantic relationship. Both carry their scars, or sometimes open wounds, from past relationships; each has their own story, their own version of reality that they have created to make sense of life. It is easy to forget that everyone creates their own version of reality. When you come into a relationship with another, it's as if, to some extent, there is an attempt to merge stories so that there is some common ground, a shared new story as well as uniqueness and differences.

THEIR LAST DAY arrived too quickly. After an afternoon on the beach, they were showered and glowing from the kiss of the sun's rays and headed into town to eat at their favourite restaurant on the main pedestrian precinct under the balmy night sky. She looked so sexy and refined at the same time with her delicate, light brown skin and her simple short, black cotton dress gathered at the waist with a broad buckled, brown leather belt. He wore a white linen shirt with his green Bermuda shorts and his bronzed skin contrasted with the newly acquired blonde streaks in his long brown hair; a gift from the Portuguese sun.

After a little deliberation, they chose from the menu and sipped their red wine from the large elegant glasses freshly poured by the smart young waiter. They were in no rush to eat as they wanted to savour their last night together. As they talked and drank in the atmosphere his eyes feasted on the beautiful woman who sat before him. For some reason, on this particular evening, she looked more stunning than ever.

"You are the most beautiful woman in the world," he told her.

She blushed and smiled at the same time.

"Thank you."

Then, as if on cue, the street seller with the red roses arrived at their table. Three roses were bought, and he handed them across the table to his sweetheart, leaning over with puckered lips to receive his payment of a kiss. The romance of the moment was inescapable. For a while they both sat silently looking at each other with bashful smiles, while the people around them carried on their business, unaware of the sacredness of the moment between these two human beings.

What a beautiful moment, what a precious moment; a moment never to come again. How our lives are full of moments, each one unique and fragile like snowflakes landing on the warm ground. Lost in our minds, we miss so many moments with our habitual attention on the past or the future. But this moment under a warm sky, with the buzz of diners around them, was divine. He did his best to drink in every aspect of it with his senses and tucked it away neatly in a small, velvet lined box in his heart where it would be safe forever.

CHAPTER 12

Their return from Portugal meant that they were both sucked into the vacuum of the busyness of their modern western lives. He did his best to leave spaces between his business commitments so that he could walk on the hills, spend time visiting friends and generally relax. He knew that he needed to find his joy of life from different sources, but he was under her spell and he only really wanted to be in her company. At times he felt disappointed that his eight-day ordeal had not purged him more deeply of his neediness and insecurity.

He often felt a slight tension in the air, but it didn't put him off; he still wanted to be with her. It seemed as if he was the only one that noticed the tension, though. He couldn't work out whether he was just making it all up in his mind. Isn't it true that often two conversations are going on when people attempt to communicate: one spoken with words and one spoken internally, within our silent thoughts? He wanted so much that when they were together, there would only ever be one conversation happening; a conversation in which there could be total honesty, where nothing was unspoken, out of bounds or taboo. And yet, he knew that his own fear of rocking the boat and triggering an emotional reaction from her meant that he didn't always share what was on his mind. Instead, he would find himself secretly fishing for clues to see if all was well with her. Her words would reassure him that she was fine, though he didn't always believe her. He knew how she disliked conflict, and his mind would convince him that she wasn't totally honest because of a fear of falling out. He wanted her to tell him if he had said something to offend her, for her to share her fears, her doubts. For him, nothing was off limits, and everything could be resolved and cleared through open, honest dialogue. But, try as they might, the goal always seemed to elude them. A glance or a pause, a certain intonation or a turning away were taken as evidence and interrogated by his ruthless and suspicious mind. He could not pretend to know what was on her mind so he would let his thoughts go as best he could, giving her the benefit of the doubt time and time again.

It seemed as if the sunny parts of their time together became fewer and more far between. The unsettled cloudy patches came around more often. They would argue over seemingly unimportant details; it was never about what was said or done, but their interpretation of words and actions. He knew his mind was trying to convince him that he should not give himself fully to this woman. Still, he noted any little piece of evidence why they would never grow old together.

And yet, when they made love, all the fear disappeared. There were many flavours to their lovemaking; wild and tempestuous, tender and gentle, primal and passionate. Afterward, regardless of how they had made love, as they lay together side by side, hand in hand, his mind always came to rest in a meadow of wildflowers where it lay on its back, looking at the tremendous sparkling blanket of stars, gently humming to itself. It was always when he was most at peace.

There were other beautiful times together, too.

One Sunday, they decided to go for a drive and on the way back they stopped at a little café that he knew. After a drink and bite to eat, he led her along a path behind the café that took them down to a secluded stretch of the river. Here the willow trees dangled the ends of their branches and leaves into the clear water as the river meandered sleepily along. The breeze caressed the leaves of the gnarled old beech at the top of the bank affectionately. His intention had not been to swim, but when they arrived the water was just too seductive and inviting.

He quickly undressed and slipped naked into the cool water while she sat on the bank and watched. He liked it that she was watching him.

It was cold, and he didn't stay in long. He returned to the bank where he dried himself a little with his shorts. He had probably wanted to impress her a little with his wild man ways. He enjoyed her attention as she chatted to him about a time when she had swum in a river in Italy, while she watched him dress. He sat beside her and the beauty of the moment, with the backdrop of the meandering river and the tangled trees and bushes, filled him to overflowing; he couldn't help but say the three simple words that he felt so strongly, "I love you."

"I love you too," she replied in an instant.

He looked at her in disbelief.

"Can you say that again?" he asked.

She gave him 'that look' but conceded to his request and repeated the words. His eyes welled up, and tears rolled down his cheeks. He had waited so long to hear those words. He felt utterly overwhelmed with joy and relief.

After a little while of just looking into her beautiful eyes, a question arose.

"When did that happen?"

She told him she had felt something stronger for him recently, and that she had begun to realise that she was in love.

"Sometimes you are so calm and loving and vulnerable, and recently I have seen this so much more than before."

Secretly, he wondered why she had not told him sooner, but he let the thought drift on. He was so relieved that she had said those three special words. Since the day on the beach in Devon when he had told her that he loved her, he had tried to convince himself that it didn't matter that she didn't love him.

He was sure that one day she would feel the same way as he did and he had resigned himself to waiting. And now the waiting was over. In his mind, he decided that he could relax. Now that she loved him, too, nothing would come between them. Like a tree on a windswept ridge, they would be able to weather any storms because the roots of their love would now just burrow deeper and deeper into the ground of their loving union. He knew that it was common for emotional issues to arise and recognised this as the healing potential of relationship. He was grateful to her for bringing his childhood trauma to the light of consciousness so that it could be transformed once and for all. He was resigned to the tumult of their twin flame dynamic and felt sure that soon they would come to the end of the rocky part of the journey and things would get smoother and easier.

He was a happy man as they walked to the car along the narrow footpath past hazel and hawthorn hedges fringed with nettles and meadowsweet.

The English summer, such as it had been, was at an end. On this day, though, the weather was warm and dry, so they decided to have a barbeque up on the hills that evening. They packed a bottle of wine, some marinated chicken, vegetarian sausages and peppers and a container of rice salad. They drove up the hill and parked, before climbing the short ascent up to their favourite spot on the ridge. From here they enjoyed the three hundred and sixty-degree view as the multi-coloured patchwork of fields stretched away in every direction to the distance of the horizon.

He lit the barbeque, and they cuddled together on the picnic blanket while the meat hissed and dripped onto the black and white charcoal, causing fatty little flares of flame and smoke to rise, before dispersing into the gentle breeze.

They talked while they ate and every now and then her body would tremble and shake with the kundalini energy. She recounted times when the energy was particularly strong, and it seemed that it was usually when she was particularly centered and still within herself. The previous week, a particularly vigorous wave of energy had happened while she was in her yoga class and she laughed when she shared how people must have thought her a little odd. But she didn't really mind, she understood enough that the body's supreme intelligence was just at work releasing and healing whatever it needed to. He felt an element of pride that this unusual phenomenon had been largely facilitated, or at least catalysed, by their coming together. It seemed to support his feeling that there was something magical and 'meant to be' about their connection. Beyond the human experience of their romantic relationship, he knew that something deeper, on a soul level, was taking place. They were catalysts for the healing of each other's souls. Perhaps they had known each other in previous lifetimes.

It was already late when they arrived on the hill. The light began to fade as they sat next to each other with full stomachs, wine in hand and the picnic blanket wrapped around their shoulders. As they looked out to the horizon, the lights of houses began to speckle the fading green landscape. They talked about the beauty and the pain of being human, about the fleeting, fragile nature of life and of the roads they had walked that had brought them to this point together now under the emerging stars.

"Make love to me," he said in a matter of fact way.

"What, here…now?" she said, looking around. "What if someone walks past?"

She seemed a little concerned, though something in her voice told him that she liked the idea. He reasoned that it was highly unlikely that they would be disturbed, as it was almost dark, and he could lie on his back so that she could sit on top with the picnic blanket around her shoulders.

"Even if someone did come past, they would be hard pressed to know what we were up to, as long as you can manage to keep relatively quiet!" he teased.

He had been right; she didn't take much convincing. After cuddling and kissing for a while, she slid her jeans and knickers off, wrapped herself in her makeshift cloak and straddled him while skillfully guiding him inside her. He lay with his hands behind his head and felt and watched her as she squirmed and writhed her hips for maximum contact and penetration. Her hair cascaded onto the blanket around her shoulders and she was framed by the darkness of the night sky, its few early stars twinkling with approval at the scene below. The tip of her tongue explored her delicate pink lips seductively, and she moaned quietly as her hips continued to move rhythmically to the silent pulse of pleasure that enveloped them both. He slid his hands up under the blanket and found the warm, gentle flesh of her breasts.

The magic of the moment brought her quickly to climax, and she did her best to stifle the sounds of delight that emanated from within, conscious still of any possible late evening walkers.

"What about you?" she asked once the waves of sweet energy had stopped rippling through her body enough so that she could speak.

"I am fine my darling, come cuddle me and wrap the blanket around us. Let's just be here quietly under the stars together."

"I love you," he said.

"And I love you, too," she replied.

The world disappeared as they lay on the earth. As they breathed together, as one, there was no past, no future, just a moment that he wanted to last forever. As the warmth of their passion began to diminish, the cold air of the descending night snuck under their blanket. Reluctantly, they left the sanctuary and beauty of the moment to seek warmth back home in the comfort of his flat.

IT WASN'T TO be long before the strength of their love was to be tested. As always, it was as if the flames of disagreement had arisen from nowhere. However, the truth was that over the recent weeks the tinder had been dried by what was unspoken between them. The usual dynamic was at play and, as he found out more about her past, he became convinced that she had serious issues around trusting men. Was this why he so rarely felt safe and secure in their connection and togetherness? Perhaps she too was always looking for reasons why she should not commit fully to the relationship. Her behaviour and comments seemed to point to this much of the time, yet, whenever issues were raised around her jealousy or trust, she would become defensive and say things like, 'certain things are just not appropriate.' This meant the conversation was over.

Although she had facilitated the release of so much of his childhood trauma during his eight-day purge, he was aware that much of what he was feeling must still be connected with his own past; this must have been what was still fueling his insecurity. Because she had her own issues, she found it hard to hold space for him when he confessed his inner turmoil and struggles. Instead, she would take his doubts and concerns personally and become cold and distant. The man in him reminded himself over and over that they would walk together as long as they were meant to, and that if she left, then he would be fine. But the emotional boy within would often cloud his rational thoughts, and he would be at the mercy of fear-driven emotions.

Jealousy was not something that visited him often but, on this occasion, it was the spark that lit the fuse.

They had been to a theatrical performance in the park near her home. He hadn't really enjoyed it at all and had only agreed to go because it was something she wanted to do. He was happy to stay in and watch movies together, to cook and talk or read, or to walk the countryside. She preferred other, more varied experiences, though.

As they drove back, he could feel an irritation rising in him. She had seemed more distant than usual. He assumed she was annoyed by his constant need for reassurance that seemed to be oozing from him again of late. As was so often the way, her demeanour had been cool and aloof when what he wanted so much was to feel warm and close.

They stopped at a petrol station, and she filled up her car and paid in the kiosk. She returned with a chocolate bar and, in a puzzled way, she said "I think that man just gave me a free chocolate bar."

Instead of feeling pleased he became instantly jealous and possessive. He knew it was ridiculous, but he felt a muffled heat and rage rising in him. 'How dare this man give her a free chocolate bar,' he thought. It was obviously because he fancied her; had she really needed to let him know about this when she must have known how he was already feeling? The severity of his response to such an innocent occurrence seemed ridiculous.

He simmered silently with rage beside her in the car as they drove the short distance back to her place. He knew that she could feel what he felt because she was an empath, too. He wished that the feelings would just disappear, but they had their hooks in him now, and his mind began to mock and jeer him with thoughts of how useless and pathetic he was.

While she prepared some food, he watched the television, and slowly his feelings began to dissolve. By the time they had eaten and watched a few programs things were sweeter between them. Nothing really had been discussed, and everything had been tidied away into the emotional store cupboard. But it would seem that the door had not been closed properly this time. The cupboard was already too full, and soon everything was to come tumbling out.

She was getting ready for bed. He was sat in bed under the covers and was supposed to be reading, but he loved watching her undress. The thought of her silky nakedness against his skin was a welcome balm to apply to the difficult emotions he could still feel from earlier. They began chatting, and she mentioned the possibility of her home being haunted as she sometimes heard strange sounds.

"What if this house is haunted and you are possessed and 'bring him home' is their way of saying 'kill him'! You don't have a knife under your pillow, do you?" he jokingly asked.

She shot a quick, sharp glance at him and hissed "That is a cruel and unwarranted and insensitive thing to say."

Her sweetness was gone in an instant, and the stab of her anger surprised him. He countered as best as he could.

"I was only joking. It just popped into my awareness, and I spoke without thinking."

He knew he should have thought before he opened his mouth, so he apologized. But it was too late. For some reason, she was severely angered by his clumsy joke. The cold wall came down again, and she was gone. He tried to reach her and reason with her; maybe it was just an overreaction on her part because of the tension between them earlier in the day, but she was adamant that it was nothing to do with this.

"If you can't see that you have massively overreacted to my clumsy joke then you are a stupid bugger!" he shouted.

His comment enraged her even more, and she turned on him with a menacing look on her face.

"Get out of my house!" she screamed. "I will not be berated and spoken to in that way."

By this time, his temper was also unleashed, and he shouted a volley of accusations at her. She was unable to communicate, emotionally unavailable and was being ridiculously over sensitive. He meant everything he said, but at the same time, he knew he should have spoken more calmly. The raising of his voice was just the excuse she needed to bring the argument to an end.

"Get out!" she yelled.

He had no choice. His feeble attempt at salvaging some semblance of control by saying that he would leave when he was ready was futile. He dressed in a hurry and threw his belongings in his bag before slamming the front door behind him.

He drove back home through the night with that all too familiar wretched feeling in his stomach. On arriving home, he curled up in his bed alone, angry and frustrated that he should find himself in this place again. It had all happened so quickly. The one consolation he had was that a friend of his was coming to stay the following day; at least there would be some distraction from his feelings that were bound to torment him. After all, how long was it going to be before she spoke to him this time?

It seemed that his main crime, the thing that had really upset her, was when he had called her a 'stupid bugger.' He felt that he had been reserved in his choice of words and that she had massively overreacted to his silly attempt at a joke. But then he remembered her history and realised that this, coupled with the unresolved tensions from the day, was probably the reason why she had overreacted so much. He knew that she would not reach out to him and that her pride would be an obstacle to her apologising even if she did see that she had been partly in the wrong. After numerous trips to the bathroom and endless cycles of turning his pillow over, sleep arrived.

IN THE MORNING, the sensation of nausea was less, and he managed a little breakfast. He got on with his day as best he could and in the evening went to the airport to collect his friend. He knew it was not a nice thing to think, but he hoped that she would be a little bit jealous knowing that he had his female friend for company. He would never be unfaithful to her, but he felt as if her reaction to his joke was much too severe for the crime that he had committed. Part of him wanted to punish her.

He decided to swallow his pride and reminded himself that it was better to be close than it was to be right, so he sent her a message by way of apology. But her response, when it came, was cold and hard. She reiterated that she was not prepared to be with anyone who spoke to her in that way and that she did not want to hear from him. He tried calling, but she didn't pick up, and so he was left in that place again of not knowing whether they were over or not.

He did his best to be clear and separate the facts from the stories his mind was busily constructing around the previous day's incident. The man in him was able to forgive her because he was sure that she had only acted from a place of unconscious pain; the boy in him was scared that she would not return.

This time, though, the emotional storm inside him was not so dense. He didn't feel anywhere near as much fear or distress as he had after Devon. He desperately wanted them to make up and be close again, but he felt a new sense of autonomy and strength because now he really believed that if she were no longer in his life, he would be just fine. He began to think that perhaps he would be better off without her, but still, he waited and waited for a text message that never came.

It was good to have his friend for company, despite the unease he felt in his body and in the back of his mind. He did his best to be a good host and, at her suggestion, they decided to go to Glastonbury for a day trip. His friend was from North America, and she wanted to experience the sights of this ancient historical place.

They had a great day, and he posted some photos of them enjoying themselves on social media. Perhaps part of his motive was to make her jealous. Regardless of his motives, it elicited a response. She sent him a message telling him that his choice of words and photos had been inappropriate. Maybe she was right; after all, two wrongs did not make a right. However, he was fed up with being stonewalled and her inability to accept her part when things went wrong. He knew that she was jealous but was too proud to admit this. After a few days, his guest left, and he was left with a sense of not knowing and an uncomfortable distance between them.

As ALWAYS, IT was him who took the lead. With the help of some carefully worded messages, she became more communicative and, after a short reconciliatory phone conversation, they agreed to meet. While he was prepared to take most of the responsibility for their latest argument, she would not accept that her response was overdramatic because of her own issues. There was nothing he could do apart from resigning himself again to the fact that maybe he did not see things clearly. He admitted that his photos posted on social media may have been insensitive, but she would give no quarter in acknowledging any jealousy. Instead, she just kept repeating that it was inappropriate, and how would he have felt if she had done the same? He knew that he might have also felt some jealousy if the tables were turned, but he was fully aware that he would admit to it rather than hide behind the rationale that it was inappropriate! He hated it when they fell out, though, so he was willing to concede again and move on.

In an attempt to delete the latest incident, he showed her two small stone hearts that he had bought for them in Glastonbury and suggested they buried them in the soil of the clematis plant that she had given him. He liked the symbolism of their two hearts together in the privacy and safety of the dark soil, and she seemed appreciative of the gesture.

But, as usual, things never really seemed fully resolved. It was if another door inside of her closed, and he wasn't allowed in that room anymore. It felt as if, one by one, the doors were slowly shutting, although he desperately tried to convince himself that this was not the case. He told himself that he was just paranoid. If she said that everything was good between them, then he needed to believe her and trust. After all, he reassured himself, she was in love with him now. Their love would be enough to equip them to face any challenges or past traumas that might arise as a result of their relationship. He knew that he wanted, once and for all, to be free of his mother related trauma and that 'bring him home' had something to do with this.

No matter how unjust she appeared to be treating him with her stonewalling, passive-aggressive tendencies, he knew that it was what he needed to dissolve the timelines of his story. That was the key to healing this old wound. He just had to keep feeling compassion for her and forgiving her for the perceived injustices that she inflicted on him. He just needed to keep his ego in check and remind himself that sometimes it was better to be close than it was to be right. She was the perfect antidote for his 'illness.' Every time she closed a little or left him or sent him away, it was an opportunity to separate the emotions elicited by the present situation from old trauma that resided in his psyche. He was prepared to suffer the discomfort of the treatment if it would finally bring him home to a place of peace after so many years. And perhaps in this place, they would be able to begin building a life together in the present without the constant presence of ghosts from the past.

The amount of emotional triggering meant that he was forced to become increasingly mindful; he noticed more and more how there was a direct connection between the thoughts that he was having and the emotions that he felt in his body. She seemed to have the power to bring him to places of deep peace and bliss and, at the same time, to cast him adrift to a place of loneliness and terror within. But he began to see that this was not entirely true. It was his thoughts and interpretation of what was going on between them that had a large part to play in how he felt. The pain of rejection at times was just so acute that he was forced to become more mindful and consciously choose thoughts that were based on the evidence before him rather than whispers and contortions of old memories.

His mindfulness practise expanded into other aspects of his life, and increasingly he would find himself in the present moment rather than lost in thoughts. The feeling of awe and wonder at the beauty of life accompanied him always on his walks under the sky. It was impossible to avoid the miracle of life when so directly confronted by the splendour of the sun, the sky, the trees, the land. But now, when he was driving or washing up or brushing his teeth, he would often soak up these more mundane moments, too. He aimed to become fully present and put all his awareness on the information coming in through his senses. He found more and more that in this place of presence there was a deep rest; often, his eyes would fill up as little waves of bliss rippled through his torso. It seemed that the powerful feelings that were arising in him were too much to be contained within his body. At times, he would emerge from these short windows of bliss and his sense of self would be gone. He would look around him and not know where he was, or who he was, for a few moments. Then, the memory would return. It was if the more fear that was cleared out of him through consciously facing the challenges of the relationship, the more he became a clear vessel for life to flow through him.

This woman was having a profound impact on him. He was so grateful, and yet at times, he was so angry with her because it was so painful. Like being on a rollercoaster ride, he had no brakes and no steering wheel! It was an exercise in surrender, in allowing himself to be tossed this way and that, like a small boat on a huge ocean. He was adrift on the ocean of love and, though at times it was so calm and serene, other times it was wild, scary and unpredictable.

Was it his love of her, or his fear of being without her that meant that he never really considered leaving? Although everything seemed to be saying otherwise, he had convinced himself that they could have a future together. Perhaps his fear of losing her meant that he just didn't want to consider that they were not destined to stay together. They say that love is blind, but what if it is fear that obscures our vision?

When they made love, the waves of bliss that had always arched his back with their intensity stopped happening. His orgasms were confined to a much smaller area around his groin. Her body also seemed to tremor much less than it used to. He wondered whether this was because there was not the same closeness as there had been, or it was possible that the kundalini energy had just done the clearing work that was needed for now. He was indeed being cleared out and, as a result, his senses became sharper and more sensitive. Colours seemed brighter, and the spectrums seemed wider. It was as if he saw the world anew through artist's eyes.

One day, something peculiar happened. He was delivering a presentation on 'The Gifts in Adversity' at a conference, based on his first autobiographical book. It was supposed to have been a weekend away for both of them, but they had argued a few days earlier, and she had said that she would not come with him. He was not feeling great, but by now he was more accustomed to this sort of thing, so he had resigned himself to the weekend without her.

Suddenly, as he was speaking to his audience, he heard a clear voice in his head taunt him. 'What are you doing? You really don't know what you are on about. You are a fraud. You should admit it, make your apologies and walk off the stage.'

A wave of crimson panic rose in him. For a moment, it was if there were three aspects of himself on the stage. The first was the one speaking the words that were coming out of his mouth. The second was the voice in his mind that was mocking him, being most unhelpful. And the third was the aspect of him that was observing the other two.

It was a peculiar and unnerving experience, but he managed to compose himself, ignore the unhelpful voice in his mind and complete his presentation. He left the stage feeling unusually hot and clammy and was grateful that the audience seemed to be totally unaware of what he had experienced.

He didn't really know what was going on, but he knew that he wasn't the same man that had met this beautiful, frustrating and mysterious woman eight months ago. He wasn't sure if he was going a little bit crazy, but he consoled himself with the knowledge that he had never really rated sanity very highly anyway!

MOST OF THE time, he felt the distance between them more than he felt the closeness. He accepted that he had no control over what was happening for her and that his task was to keep letting go of any fear around losing her and just enjoy the time they had together. He had asked if they could meet up more often in the week and this did happen occasionally, but between them, their lives seemed to be too busy to accommodate another evening just to be together. He felt sure that if he saw her during the week, there would be less space for his mind to get up to mischief because the critical and fear-based thoughts were always strongest when they were not together. He knew that his little boy was responsible for the mischief and was constantly seeking reassurance that all was well, mainly because it was obvious that in some ways it was not and their togetherness was uncertain. He would speak regularly with his mentor about his internal processes and, though he would always leave feeling clearer and optimistic, it would not be long before small gangs of marauding, destructive thoughts were clamouring for his attention again.

It didn't help that she was always so tired, either. Good nights of sleep continued to elude her, which resulted in her being more controlling and emotional. But she was doing her best, and he knew this. Despite her tiredness, it was her turn to surprise him, and she booked a weekend away for them both. He wasn't supposed to know where they were going, but his mind-reading skills were becoming alarmingly good; to her amazement, he knew the event that she had tickets for straight away.

The journey down was fine. As always, he enjoyed having her in the car with him. He still felt that sense of pride because she was the most gorgeous woman in the world to him. He wanted to be seen with her. He liked the fact that it was just him and her in the car. They had talked about introducing each other to their friends, but somehow there never seemed to be time, and the truth was that when he saw her, he wanted her all to himself.

He would still place her hand on his thigh while they were driving for some physical connection. Usually, this was enough for him to feel aroused. He wanted to ask her to unzip his trousers and fondle him while they drove, but for some reason, he held his tongue. It was probably that old fear of rejection, or maybe he didn't want her to fully know that he was hungry for her so much of the time.

They arrived at the bed and breakfast that she had booked; in fact, the whole break was her treat. She had planned and arranged as a thank you for the weekend that he had arranged when they had visited the art gallery in Yorkshire. He was touched by her thoughtfulness. Although she was sometimes high maintenance, he couldn't help but be impressed by so many of her lovely qualities. She was kind, generous, intelligent, had a great sense of humour and a big heart, even it was a little guarded at times.

After unpacking quickly, they headed into town to get their bearings and have a look around. She complained that she was a little tired, but they thought nothing of it as this was often the case.

Later, while she got ready to go out, he answered a few emails on his phone and scrolled through his social media platforms. He liked the care that she took to get ready to go out; applying some subtle shades of makeup, combing and arranging her hair until she was happy with it and choosing her clothes. Sometimes she would ask him to choose between two outfits. He always found the choice difficult. To distract attention from his struggle to choose he would always say "Darling, you will look gorgeous in either outfit, but you always look your best for me when you are naked."

This wasn't totally true. He liked to see her semi-naked in her underwear best. She was most arousing to his eyes in her knickers and bra, but as soon as she was within reach, he wanted total naked flesh; nothing to hinder the movement of his fingers over her heavenly, smooth skin.

Unfortunately, there wasn't time to make love, and they made their way back into town to a restaurant that had caught her eye. She had a girlish excitement about her, which often emerged when they were out. She mentioned again how she was really looking forward to the concert. So was he, but almost as soon as he sat down at the restaurant his nose started running, and he found himself amid a strange allergic reaction to something. He tried not to make a fuss about it, and he did his best to enjoy the food while blowing his nose repeatedly. When they left the restaurant, the symptoms subsided, and they made their way to the music venue.

But it became apparent that she was a little uncomfortable at the concert. It was a little wilder and unconventional than she was used to. The music was an unusual mixture of African and English folk music with a very catchy beat. He wanted to move to the front of the crowd and dance, but she seemed nervous and wanted to stay at the edge, which irritated him a little. He had drunk a beer or two by this time so his empathy wasn't quite what it could be. Eventually, she agreed to move deeper into the crowd. He held her from behind closely while they swayed and bounced to the rhythms and beat. All too soon the last song had been played, and they made their way back to their room for the night.

As they arrived back, she mentioned that she didn't feel quite right. She must have read the expression on his face because she quickly added, "I think I am well enough to make love, though."

"Are you sure?" he asked; though a weekend away without sex would be like tonic without gin.

They began to make love tenderly, but it was clear that she wasn't feeling great.

"Would you like me to stop?" he asked.

"No carry on, darling, I am fine," she replied.

He knew he could have stopped, but he was close to climax and so enjoying the intimacy of the moment. She seemed especially delicate and vulnerable this night, so he was as gentle as possible and soon he was kissing her belly.

They lay beside each other in their unusual surroundings. Before too long, she rolled over onto her side and said goodnight. He kissed her on the shoulder and settled himself under the covers, listening to her breathing get softer and slower until he knew she was asleep. He always thought it was such an honour that she felt safe enough to fall asleep naked and vulnerable beside him. He lay listening to the hum of the mini fridge and occasional cars passing in the distance. Before long, he too was asleep.

HE WAS AWOKEN by the sound of her coughing and spluttering beside him.

"Darling, I feel terrible," she whispered. Her throat was sore, and she had a splitting headache.

"O bless," he crooned, stroking her hair.

"I need to go home," she said. "I want my bed."

Pretty soon they were on the road heading back up the motorway. He tried to persuade her to stay with him so that he could care for her, but she was adamant that she needed to get back home because she was feeling worse and worse by the minute. She had left her car at his place, and when they arrived, he put her case into the boot of her car before giving her a hug and a kiss on the forehead. She climbed gingerly into her car, closed the door, turned the key in the ignition and drove off.

He felt sorry for her, but he couldn't help feeling disappointed that their precious time together had been cut short. He had wanted her to let him look after her while she felt unwell, though at the same time he did understand her preference to go to her own home and bed.

The next day he discovered by text message that she had come down with a severe dose of the flu. Over the coming week, she got progressively worse and worse. He didn't want her to suffer, and he hoped he would still be able to see her the following weekend even if she was not feeling great.

He wanted to go and visit her, to look after her, but she would have none of it. The best he managed was that she conceded to the occasional short phone call. But the phone calls were not enough, and the conversations felt stilted, as he tried his best not to convey any of the sadness and rejection that he felt in his heart. He knew that she wasn't feeling great, but his empathy failed him. He kept thinking that if he had been feeling unwell, he would have still liked to see her. In the distance between their connection, more seeds of fear and doubt began to sprout and take root. Every little fearful thought he had ever had about losing her became magnified as the days of her illness turned into weeks. He knew it was crazy and did his best to stay with the facts and focus on his work. He told himself that she was just ill and didn't want him to see her in such a vulnerable place. But the demons in his mind taunted him, insisting that this unwillingness to let him in was further evidence that she would never be his.

After three weeks, she was feeling significantly better and agreed to him coming to visit. He was overjoyed and reassured her that he would expect nothing of her and that she was beautiful to him however rough she felt or looked.

He arrived, and they made some simple food together and cuddled up to watch a film on the sofa. The atmosphere did not feel great. He knew that she knew that he had felt excluded and pushed away during her illness, but neither of them wanted to talk about it.

Later, when they were both naked in bed, she asked him to make love to her tenderly. He was more than happy to oblige. He smiled inwardly because he knew she was partly asking because she knew how much he wanted it after not seeing each other for so long.

The next morning, they set off for a gentle walk across the fields. Before long, though, the conversation became a little heated. He hadn't planned to mention it at all, but he found himself commenting on her lack of communication while she had been unwell. This led to other unresolved issues being raised and in no time at all they had a full-blown argument. The more he tried to get her to see things from his perspective, the more she dug her heels in and disappeared behind her invisible ice shutter.

And then it happened. He should have seen it coming. He should have trusted his own judgment when he felt her disappearing further and further away from him and not convinced himself that he was just making things up in his insecure mind.

"I can't do this any longer," she said. "I have had enough. It's over. We just argue all the time, and I don't want to do this anymore."

"But you told me that you love me," he protested feebly.

"I thought I did, but as the weeks went by and you kept being so needy and insecure, I realised that I didn't love you."

"Well, that's just great," he said, aghast, "you could have told me."

"I was going to-" she countered, but he had already interrupted her.

"That's bloody typical, isn't it? You were going to, but you never got around to it. Perhaps if you didn't have so many bloody communication issues we wouldn't be where we are now!" he shouted.

She shot him a vicious look, and he knew that he had said too much. There was no coming back from this argument.

With one last feeble attempt at reconciliation, he asked "Are you sure it's over?"

It seemed a ridiculous question, bearing in mind all the doubts that he had been feeling over the recent weeks.

"I just can't do this anymore. It's not working, can't you see that?"

"I know it's difficult at the moment because you have been ill. We just haven't seemed to find the time to be together or talk or connect properly."

And then he remembered: she didn't love him. Perhaps she never had. Or, maybe she didn't have a clue what love was. Perhaps he didn't, either.

She stood with her back to him, looking over the fields and hedges and he knew that it was over.

"Okay," he said. "I will go."

And so, he did. He walked quickly back to her house and packed up his few things into his overnight bag. By the time she arrived back, he was leaving to get into his car.

"Can I have a hug?" she said. "I never meant to hurt you."

"No, you can't have a hug, I'm afraid. It would just hurt too much."

As he walked down the steps with his bag, he turned to look at her. She was stood framed in the beech doorway looking as beautiful as ever. A part of him crumpled inside.

"It's a funny old thing, life, isn't it?" he said to her out of the open car window.

He didn't know why he said it, the words just slipped out of his mouth. He pulled out into the road, taking one more, quick glance before driving away.

CHAPTER 13

It was a miserable drive back home. He was devastated. This time it really was over, she had made herself very clear. All that his mind wanted to focus on were all the beautiful times that they might have had together that would never come to pass. The lorries and cars on the motorway were just noisy shapes; everything lacked colour. He knew this place. He traveled through a grey world back to his flat.

On arriving home his heavy legs carried him down the steps, and he unlocked the door. He was back safely, but the usual feeling of homecoming was denied; instead, his uninhabited flat only accentuated the loneliness that he felt inside. He wished that she had never come to his home because memories of her seemed to be everywhere.

He video called her on his mobile phone. He couldn't help himself. He thought that perhaps it was all a terrible mistake and that she might already regret what she had done. It was all too sudden. Hadn't he asked her to speak to him if something was not right between them? Hadn't he changed as she had asked him to? He had never raised his voice to her again after the 'stupid bugger' incident. It didn't seem fair that she had made the decision without him. It wasn't grown up; it wasn't meant to end like this. He was relieved that she took his call, but as he listened to what she had to say, her polite, but cold demeanour confirmed to him that she was gone. There was no warmth, no softness. The woman that he loved was not there anymore. He knew this place, too - the other side of a thick wall where he could see her but couldn't reach her. She had closed the final part of her heart to him to protect herself. They said goodbye amicably enough, and he pressed the red button on his phone, and she was gone.

He stood a moment in shock and then collected his thoughts. There was work to be done. The place was full of memories of their togetherness. It was haunted by her ghost. In the kitchen, he saw the back of her as she stood in front of the sink, washing up the breakfast dishes while they chatted, and he admired her bum. In the living room, the sofa taunted him with images of her sitting on top of him, her head thrown back, throat exposed, and her unkempt, wild hair swept back while they made love. There were no sounds, he heard nothing, the movie was a silent one, but the images were clear, and he began to cry. As he passed the bathroom, he saw her naked in the shower. He looked behind him and saw her angelic face and her effervescent smile while she stood in the doorway of the lounge in jeans and T-shirt.

He moved as quickly as he dared to the bedroom; the love stained bed sheets were cruel, and he pulled them off hurriedly. He thought he caught a faint smell of her as he went about his work and his awareness returned to the dull sensation in his chest that was now an intense ache. He bundled the linen into the washing machine as fast as he could and turned it on as waves of grief flooded over him and tears rolled down his face.

Next, he went to the drawer where she kept her toiletries, cosmetics and some personal effects. He had always loved this drawer because it would remind him that she would be back in between their times together. Sometimes, when he was missing her acutely, he would look inside and breathe in the smell of face cream which emanated from the drawer and reminded him of her. It reassured him that soon she would once again be in his arms, that she was not a dream.

But today was a different story. He put some of the contents of the drawer into the dustbin and others into a carrier bag to take to the charity shop. He didn't want it in his home. On the hook behind the bedroom door was her dressing gown, white, soft and fluffy. He held it against his face and inhaled the fragrance of her, knowing that it would probably be for the last time.

He knew that he couldn't erase all memories of her from his home, but he had to do something that would give him hope that this pain would not last indefinitely. He needed a glimmer of hope that life would once again be bearable and that his grief would not last forever.

Once he had finished removing everything that was hers, he scanned the flat again and then allowed his body to sink wearily into the chair at his desk. He gazed vacantly out of the window while the computer loaded up and he allowed the waves of sadness to wash over him.

He deleted all their emails and photos from his phone, and then her contact details. He knew he would be able to contact her if he wanted to.

With a deep breath, he opened the folder on his computer where photographs were kept. Tears blurred his vision, and he wiped them away with his sleeve to focus on the task ahead. He opened every folder with pictures of her; memories of places they had been together, moments in time that would never be again. One by one he hit the delete button until there were only nine left. These were the ones where she looked the most beautiful and held the most precious memories; on the hills, in Portugal at the restaurant, the village in Yorkshire, on the bench outside his flat. Every photograph revealed a different facet of her: gentle, kind, pure, arrogant, sexy, shy, powerful, otherworldly. He created a folder which he named 'Blessings' and dragged and dropped the photos in. After emptying the recycle bin he turned the computer off and collapsed onto the sofa, while the tears still rolled down his face. His aloneness felt total.

He knew that to fully let her go he would have to feel the fullness of his grief. At the same time, though, he was already able to remind himself that nothing really was lost. She would always be a part of him. Their journey had come to an end, but the beauty of their time together would be forever woven into the fabric of his being. He was changed, and so was she. He was not the same man that she had met for the first time in the author fair or the pub all those months ago. He had allowed her to enter him fully, more than he had ever allowed any woman before. There were times when they had merged when the separateness of two individuals had blurred. These were the times when they had laid together naked, with their mouths almost touching, looking silently into each other's eyes, one breath shared between them, inhaling and exhaling as they breathed each other in and out. The mystical union and transformational energy of sacred sexuality had certainly worked its magic.

When there were no more tears left, a gentle calm began to descend upon him. After a while, he pulled himself up from the sofa and wandered around doing the mundane things that needed to be done. The world did not care about his pain and tomorrow would be a Monday; he had work to do.

As he guided himself around the flat, he was constantly reminded of her. It wasn't that he was intent on removing every trace of her, he knew this was impossible. It wasn't that he was angry with her or hated her suddenly, but he needed to do what he could to heal the nagging ache in his heart. He knew that this pain would be his companion until he could relinquish all the hope that they might be together again. There were some beautiful gifts that she had bought him, among them the ornate Moroccan tea-light holder that hung from the ceiling in the corner. There was also the clematis she had bought that they had planted together. It had grown rapidly up the trellis outside the patio doors of his bedroom. She always used to check on its progress and whisper words of encouragement to it when she arrived on Saturday evenings. These things could stay, just as he knew a part of her would always remain with him.

Slowly, the time ticked by as he lay on his bed, trying to stay focused on the movie he was watching. He began to feel the beginnings of tiredness creep in. He was scared to turn the light off too early because he didn't want to lay awake in the dark for ages, tormented by 'what ifs' and 'if only's.' When he could hardly keep his eyes open any longer, he shut down the computer and turned off the light. He lay down in the darkness and, for a moment, he couldn't help but imagine her curled up in her bed, on her left side with her knees tucked up, in the position that she always slept. He whispered goodnight to her since there would be no more goodnight texts and, before long, sleep was merciful and carried him away so that he might rest.

WHEN HE RETURNED home from his meetings the next afternoon, he felt ready for the next stage in letting her go. Buried in the soil of the clematis pot were the two small, stone hearts. He parted the cool, damp earth to reveal where he had placed them, overlapping, lying together in their earthy womb. He took them in his shaky hands, wiped them clean and placed them in his pocket. He drove up to the hills where he parked the car and began the steep climb up the path onto the ridge with one heart in each hand. Slowly, they absorbed his warmth. They felt smooth and pleasing to the touch, in stark contrast to his thoughts. His mind insisted on reminding him of various beautiful moments they had shared together on the hills under the sky, and he did his best to keep returning to the feeling of gratitude for what they had shared. The truth was that it was time to let her go. She didn't want him anymore, so their work was done. He was reminded of the twin flame video that they had watched, how for most people the intensity of the journey was too much.

On reaching the top, he removed his shoes and socks. He wanted to feel the cold, reassuring strength of the earth beneath his feet. He walked steadily forward, turning the stones in his hands, now acutely aware of their separateness with one in each hand. As he approached what had been their special spot where they had sat and talked and eaten and made love, he half expected to see her as he had once before. But she was not there and, though the ground was not bare, the cold emptiness of the place seemed to mock his foolish wish to be with her once again. In the middle of the small hollow lay some roses that had mysteriously arrived; nine red ones and three white ones. He arranged them carefully and, after kissing each stone gently, he lay the two stone hearts side by side beneath the flowers, making sure that they did not touch.

He looked out at the distant horizon and once again allowed the desolate feelings of grief to wash over him. When he was ready, he put his shoes and socks back on, returned to his car and drove the winding road back down the hill home.

When he looked back over their time together, it seemed as if she had left him a hundred times, perhaps so that this final leaving would not be so difficult. But the constant reminders of her absence pierced him time and time again, like a blunt dagger, and they forced him to feel his aloneness. He would glance at the time and remember that she would be leaving for work now, or getting ready for bed, or that she would be at her yoga class. For the first few weeks, seven o'clock on Saturday evenings were hard, for that was the time that her arrival would be imminent. The bottle of gin that he had bought for her visits taunted him from the cupboard. The cinnamon that he sprinkled on his porridge had been bought by her. He didn't know what to do with the two extra pillows that he now had so he just stuffed them under the bed. When he returned home from work, he would always catch himself glancing hopefully, ridiculously, to see if her little green car was there. Sometimes, in the evening as he lay alone on the bed watching something on his laptop, he would hear a sound. His heart would skip a beat at the foolish thought that maybe she had changed her mind and had come to pay him a surprise visit.

In the spaces between busyness he wondered what she was doing; if she was hurting, too. He didn't want her to, but at the same time, he did. He wanted to know that he had meant a lot to her, even though it now seemed that their growing old together had only ever been a silly dream. He wondered if the hurting felt the same for her as it did for him. He didn't want her to forget him.

Little by little, as the days merged together, the pain ebbed away, and the vividness of the memories of her gradually began to fade. He found peace from his grieving by being with his friends, but even then, he was not always allowed the respite of being able to forget her. One time, while deep in conversation, his friend's mobile rang. It was the same ringtone that he had assigned to her phone number. He felt the uncomfortable sinking in his stomach at the new cruel thought that he may never again hear her voice. But this thought was soon followed by the recollection of the times when he had so desperately wanted her to be more open and honest and vulnerable; how, towards the end, they had rarely met in that place that was so precious to him. Occasionally, remembering the painful times made him angry, and he noticed that somehow making her wrong made it a little easier to let her go. But he didn't want to make her wrong. Neither of them was wrong. They had just run their course, and he was grateful for all that she had brought into his life. He didn't measure the success of the relationship by its longevity, but by the depth of experience that had been shared while they were together; they had traveled deep with amazing moments of beauty, and then, of course, there was the massive purging, learning, and healing that had taken place.

By and by, amidst the jumble of mental chatter, a clear thought arose in his mind. He really needed to let her go fully. It did not feel right that their stone hearts were lying side by side on the hill. He walked most days alone on the hills, and when he arrived at the special place, everything was as he had left it. He scooped the wilted roses up and lay them in the undergrowth where they could decompose privately now that their beauty was faded. He took one heart and placed it in his pocket and the other he carried up to a small rocky crag. He kissed it one more time and lay it down by itself. She had always loved the windy places, and this little peak felt like a beautiful final resting place for her heart.

The other heart he took home and placed lovingly in the lap of the wooden, hand-carved Buddha that his friend had brought him back from Nepal. Their hearts were no longer together.

CHAPTER 14

Time continued to move slowly. Some days were more difficult than others, and he often found himself counting down the hours to when he could be enveloped by the sanctuary and relief of sleep. The nights seemed to pass too quickly; just as sleep had taken him, he would find himself awake again. On the difficult mornings, he laid under the warmth of his duvet with the morning stirring through the open window. He would do his best not to attach to the unhelpful thoughts that would often arise in an attempt to perpetuate his suffering. When time would no longer permit him to hide under the duvet, he would throw back the cover with a heavy heart at the prospect of another long day stretched before him.

Other days were easier, especially when he had a busy day and was out and about at meetings. The distraction was welcome, but on closing the door as he arrived home, the intense sadness would hit him. Thoughts would arrive to torture him like how he would never again hear the pad of her feet coming down the steps on a Saturday evening. Whenever time permitted, he would lay himself down on the bed and allow himself to feel the strange sensations of grief and loss in his heart and solar plexus. He would bring his attention to his breath and whisper her quiet blessings of gratitude and release until the intensity of the discomfort diminished.

Every day that he could, he would walk the land. This was crucial in making the grief more bearable. At times he was angry with himself that he had shared so much of his world with her, but the memory of their golden times together in nature would painfully dissolve his anger, and he would forgive himself for sharing his beauty spots with her. He had shared so much of himself in so many ways, that he had nothing to regret. He had certainly done his best and given all that he could.

BEFORE THEY HAD parted on the last day that he saw her, he had said that he didn't want to be in touch. He wanted a clean break to try and facilitate the healing process. They had agreed that if they wanted to get in touch at any point, they would be able to via Facebook Messenger. After a couple of weeks, he wrote to her.

He had been speaking with a friend who had recounted a story from his own relationship of a time when his partner had said that their time together was over and that he needed to go. His friend had refused to go, and in time they had worked things out.

He wondered if she had just been testing him and that it was possible that he had given in too easily. What if she wanted him to fight for her and prove how much he really wanted to be with her? Perhaps he should have said 'let's give it some time and space'? But he hadn't; instead, he had just left. He was aware that this wasn't the first time that something like this had happened to him. Maybe he should have done as his friend had and reminded her of their commitment to each other? Hadn't they talked about how things would come up to challenge their commitment and that, if they just stayed together, they could weather any storm? He just needed to make sure that he had done all he could in case the future brought a sense of regret and uncertainty that he had let something beautiful go too easily.

He wrote one short sentence. 'Hello. Would you like to talk?'

Her response was kind and gentle, but she declined the offer on the basis that to talk so soon might be unsettling for both. She was right, of course. It would be unsettling, but he was no longer afraid of being unsettled. Her words made it clear that she had walked away, she was sure. She was gone. He needed to read her words a few times to let a deeper sense of closure permeate its way inside him.

As the first few weeks passed, time slowly began to work its healing magic. He busied himself as best as he could with his work and other matters of consequence in his life, but he could not write properly. He had lost his muse. The words just didn't flow, and he resigned himself to networking and marketing and the more administrative aspects of his career for the time being. He was grateful for the small sum of savings he had, which he began to rely on.

The first weekends without her were the most difficult. He missed their physical intimacy, their lovemaking, and her companionship. He knew that he was remembering it all through rose-tinted spectacles; the truth was that it had been one hell of a journey. In time the awareness grew that with every ending comes a new beginning. He would be just fine. He was already fine; maybe he was just falling out of love.

He knew that he would never be the same man that he had been before she had broken open his heart. He had never loved anyone with the courage and intensity with which he had loved her. He had thought that all he needed to do was to commit fully and that would be the crucial ingredient for success. He had not entertained the idea that she might not fully commit to him, that she might not fall in love with him, that her fear and his fear might come between them. He had found her so beautiful; the attraction to her was so strong that he hadn't really considered the possibility that they might not be compatible. He had always known she was a slippery fish, that she was not a safe bet, that loving her was a risk. He had been as a moth to the flame, only he was alive, he had survived her flame, and a new man was emerging slowly from the fire of transformation. Slowly, a new, unfamiliar sense of aliveness began to rise as the grief faded; an aliveness that was richer than he could ever remember experiencing before.

But, all the time in the background, the words 'Bring him home', still haunted him.

Was he home? Was this really it or had she abandoned him without fulfilling her mission? Had she imagined the voices? Was there something he was missing, something that he wasn't seeing clearly? Some say that home is where the heart is, and he could certainly feel his heart now like he had never done before. It felt as if it had a very thorough attunement!

'But what good is it being home if there is no one to share a home with?' he thought.

And then, in a moment of transcendence, he remembered how, in truth, he was never alone. Coming home was about realising this fully. Arriving at a place of peace with himself where he could honour and enjoy his solitude was a profound gift and blessing.

He sat down at his laptop and quickly began typing some words as they rushed into his awareness.

The All One Tree

Can you see the tree that stands alone on the hill?

How complete she seems unto herself as you hurry by.

But slow down, pause a while and look again.

See how her sure branches reach and merge with the light infinity of the sky.

See how she makes love with the gentle breeze; caressed and fondled she whispers her delight in the shimmering of her delicate leaves.

See how the sun warms her, and the frost adorns her; different lovers who come to be with her a while.

How the raindrops fall upon her, trickling down her branches and trunk into the soil to be drunk by her and released again into the sky to reunite with the shapeshifter clouds that float effortlessly by.

Her leaves practise their alchemy breathing in and breathing out. Silently, unobtrusively wanting no applause or recognition she stands humbly performing her magic.

If you wait a while, you will see how the buzzard comes to rest a while in the safety of her branches to look out on the majesty of creation.

You will see how the finches and sparrows come to dine on the small creatures that have made their homes in the folds and sinews of her woody bark.

The squirrels that scamper and chase along her elevated highways and the mice curled in their cosy nest in the folds where her roots meet her trunk.

When the cold days come, she rests and relaxes and her leaves and energy fall,

Down, down, down into her roots that twist and turn, held as they are, embraced in the cool darkness of the sacred earth.

Can you see the tree that stands alone on the hill?

Look a little closer, a little deeper, a little more slowly with the eyes of your heart.

And she will remind you that you are never really alone.'

The spell was broken. It was the first surge of pure creativity that had arisen in him since they had separated.

As he looked out from the window into the greyness of the day, a robin landed on the bird table and stood for a moment, looking straight at him. It was December 21st, the Winter Solstice, the shortest day of the year; a time to embrace the mystery and magic of darkness. And yet, in that moment, he became very aware that it is also the day in which the scales tip and the lighter, longer days begin their slow return. Through the trees, he saw how the pale sun seemed to struggle to climb enough to light the sky and warm the air even a little. But his recent burst of creativity had kindled a spark of inspiration, and he watched his mind play with his idea for a moment like a cat playing with a mouse.

He clapped his hands, and the cat and mouse ran away.

"Perhaps there is room for one more love story in the world," he said out loud to himself.

In that moment he knew what his next book would be; he had to write their story. After all, she had said so many times how she loved reading the words that he wrote to her. She told him that he was a talented writer, that he should keep writing books.

He brought a candle from the coffee table and placed it on his desk. He lit it while whispering a quiet prayer as he always did before he began writing.

He pulled his laptop towards him and opened it. He looked at the empty white electronic page before him and took a long slow breath in, then exhaled silently. His fingers slowly began their gentle tapping dance across the keyboard while he watched the letters turn into words, and then sentences, that arrived on the screen in front of him.

CHAPTER 15

The book began to emerge. There was always resistance to sitting down and beginning to write because the emotions that arose while he wrote were so intense. It became a labour of love; a bittersweet catharsis. When he wrote about their lovemaking, he was filled with sadness that he would never travel those sacred realms with her again. The arousal he felt in his body as he relived the details of their lovemaking was torturous, but he knew that it needed to be captured. He wanted men and women to know how beautiful, how sacred the act of lovemaking could be. For him, it was one of the greatest gifts of being in a human body. He wanted to inspire others to experience the beauty and reverence for lovemaking that he knew.

When he wrote of the difficult times together, he was filled with sadness and remorse and wished that he could have done things differently. He relived the pain, knowing that as he felt it fully while he wrote, it would be released from his body so that all residual emotions connected to the experiences would no longer remain. Sometimes as he wrote he wished that he could have remained in his center more often and not allowed fear to trigger him and cause him to say things that he wished he had not. At other times he was a little angry with her for how she had behaved, but he knew that she had always done her very best, too. They both had. There were things that she was not able to see at the time, perhaps because of denial and because they were too painful for her to acknowledge. We don't tend to receive information that we are not yet ready to receive. What we are ready to internalise and realise is always dependent on where we are in the evolution of our soul's human journey.

We do our best to live with integrity and honesty. However, we are constantly challenged in this endeavour by the limitations and twists and turns of our individual minds that spin and weave their own stories until, ultimately, we believe they are true. It seems that it is only with the eyes of the heart that we see or feel clearly and that pain, when applied consciously, can be one of the best ways to cleanse the lens of the heart so that we can more accurately discern what is true and what is not.

He had hoped that writing the book would banish her from his mind and that, when it was finished, there would be a sense of completion in his grief. It was atonement, an exorcism and a contribution to humanity's evolution all in one.

But, as the words arrived on the screen turned into pages, something came to his attention. He knew that she was a very private person and he was aware that he could not really share the book with the world without her blessing. He began to realise that he would need to let her know what he was doing. It was something he didn't want to do by writing or over the phone. He knew that he needed to do this face to face. The idea filled him with fear and excitement. Fear at how she might react because he didn't know what he would do if she insisted that he abandon his project. And the excitement that he might see her again. Did he really need to let her know, or was it just an excuse so that he could be with her once more? He concluded that it was a bit of both. He had already thought carefully about preserving her anonymity, but he still wanted her blessing. If it were to be a book that had the potential to heal the wounds between man and woman, then the energy would have to be clear between them. It wouldn't feel right if he were to share the energy of their story without her consent.

At first, he thought that he would contact her about it on their anniversary, Valentine's Day, but then he decided that this was inappropriate and would make it too obvious to her how much he still felt for her. The more he thought about meeting, the more the possibility of making love with her again became a recurring fantasy that distracted him at regular intervals through his days. What was it about this woman? It had almost been three months since he had been with her. Gradually, the pain had receded, and he had found new contentment in his aloneness that he had not known before. Nevertheless, a part of him was ready to dive straight back in and risk his new found peace for one night of passion with her.

As a result of a conversation with his mentor, he decided that he would contact her the day after Valentine's Day and tell her that there was something that he needed to talk to her about. He was happy with his decision. She would know by the timing of his communication that he remembered the beginning of their epic journey, but he didn't want it to feel too romantic. The day after Valentine's seemed to give a clearer, if not totally honest, message.

The fourteenth of February arrived, and he felt a little sadness when he remembered the messages and poem that had been exchanged a year before. He felt what he needed to feel, knowing that he would only have to wait one more day before he could contact her. He told himself that he was crazy, but he couldn't deny the excitement that arose at the thought of possibly seeing her and the fear at how she might respond to the news that he had to share with her. There was something else, too. It felt that during their time together she was in the driving seat most of the time. Somehow, the writing of this book put him in the driving seat and, for once, he wielded some sort of power over her. He was a little uncomfortable with this; nevertheless, the feeling was there.

He was in the kitchen preparing some food when he heard the familiar Facebook message ping from his laptop. He finished what he was doing and wandered into the lounge to check the message. His heart skipped a beat when he saw that it was from her. Before he even read the words he knew that she still had feelings for him; otherwise she would not have gotten in touch on that particular day.

Her message was short and sweet, and she asked how he was. He responded to her question and wasted no time in getting straight to the point. He didn't want to get into a lengthy exchange of messages and asked if she would be prepared to meet as he had something to share. She said that she needed time to think about it, which made him laugh out loud. Immediately, he was thrown back into that familiar place of not knowing and waiting for her to let him know. It was good for him to be reminded.

But he knew that she wasn't really a game player, she just liked to think things through carefully and slowly. The next day she messaged to say that she was prepared to meet. Pretty soon a lunch meeting was agreed at a pub near him.

His excitement levels rose, and his mischievous mind alerted him straight away to the fact that since they were meeting near his place, it would be easy for them to pop back to the comfort of his flat. She had said that she didn't really like the pubs around where she lived, but he chose to interpret her choice differently. He knew that their journey together was not yet done and, more importantly, he had a good sense that he would make love with her again.

As the days passed by, his desire for her intensified. He kept reminding himself that they were meeting so that he could tell her about the book. It was possible that she might be furious with him and leave upset and angry. In his head, though, he was already making love to her. No matter how often he admonished his mind for its arousing content, his desire for her remained alarmingly powerful.

ON THE DAY of their meeting, he spent much too long choosing what to wear. He didn't have many options, but it seemed important. In the end, he decided to wear the black shirt that he knew she liked, which he had worn on their first date. He stood in front of the mirror, deciding whether to have one button undone or two. He wanted her to feel desire for him again, but he didn't want her to know how much he wanted her to desire him!

His newly washed hair dried in the cold air of the open car window as he drove to the pub where they had agreed to meet. She had not arrived yet, and he decided to wait in the car park for her. He was nervous and excited, and his heart began racing as he saw her approach in her little green car. She saw him, and when her car was parked, she walked over with her familiar confident swagger. To his equal pleasure and despair, she looked gorgeous. Her sweet angelic face delighted him and yet, unsurprisingly, it was her curvaceous hips and thighs that drew his attention most. They embraced long and slow, and much was communicated between their bodies as they stood folded around each other in the cold air of the car park. He could feel that she had missed him and that she was no longer angry with him. In that moment he knew then that he would not be spending the night alone. He breathed her in and prayed that his intuition was right.

And then, right on cue, his mind rushed in, and he feared that he was perhaps imagining things. The conversation was a little awkward as if it was the first date, but somehow he enjoyed the uncomfortableness. He enjoyed her shy glances and giggles and the twinkle in her clear blue eyes as they caught up with each other's news and family matters.

When they had eaten, he asked her if she was ready to hear the reason why he had wanted to meet. She immediately looked a little nervous but agreed that now was as good a time as any.

"I am writing a book," he said.

"Oh, that's wonderful," she exclaimed with a beaming smile.

"It's about us," he added.

Her hand rose up to cover her mouth as she gasped audibly. Her eyes shot a terrified look across the table at him.

"I feel sick," she said. "I am sorry, but I need to go to the bathroom."

She hurriedly left the table, and he sat in silence for a moment, drinking in the details of what had just happened. He summoned the waiter and paid the bill, realising that it was much too public a place for her to be while she was feeling so upset.

She returned looking a little more composed, and he helped her on with her coat, and they walked out to the car park. Under the sky he held her in silence and, gradually, she relaxed into his embrace.

"I am sorry," he said, "but I just know I have to write this book."

He tried to reassure her that he was concerned about her feelings regarding what was acceptable to share with the world, and what was not. He explained that there were people who needed to know the healing potential of relationship, about the beauty and magic that is possible. There was so much disharmony between men and women that he felt that it would be selfish not to share the riches of their incredible journey together.

"If our story might make a positive difference to one other person, then it is worth writing. I am not angry with you, and my intention is not to portray you in a bad light. On the contrary, I am so grateful for all the pain that you have gifted me with, it facilitated my journey home."

She still looked too shocked to speak and was shivering a little.

He suggested they get out of the cold and that, unless she had any other ideas, the best place for them to go would probably be his place. They could talk, and he would do his best to put her mind at ease.

He was sorry that she was so alarmed, and he didn't want her to be upset and in pain. He had known that she would probably find the idea challenging but, faced with her response, he doubted his integrity for a moment. But he knew, he really knew, that he had to write this book, it wasn't really up to him. The words somehow needed to come through him. After all, he was a writer.

As these conflicting thoughts raced through his mind, he was acutely aware that this woman who he felt so attracted to was coming back to his flat, and he was crazy with desire for her.

As she descended the steps to his flat, she burst into tears. He held her again, and between the sobs, she explained that it was so painful to be back. He reassured her tenderly and patiently, and soon they were inside with hot cups of tea in their hands.

He was genuinely concerned about her reaction to the book, but he hoped that she would feel better about it in time. He made some suggestions of how she could be involved in the editing and how he would make sure that it was one hundred percent anonymous. Gradually, the worried look on her face softened a little, and she relaxed.

The conversation moved on, and they both spoke very openly and vulnerably about the process of letting go of what they had been through. She sat on the floor with her back resting against the sofa, her tea cupped in her delicate fingers with light blue painted nails.

They talked, and talked, the minutes turned to hours. He sat on the armchair by his desk and at one point, while they spoke gently of how things had fallen apart, she began to sob once again. He beckoned her over, and she came and sat at his feet with her arm resting on his thigh. Jolts of electric passion ran through him at her touch on such a sensitive place, and his head went dizzy. His stomach became light and fuzzy.

For a while, they sat quietly together, and it was as if they had never been apart. He knew that she would never have been so intimate if she did not still have feelings for him. He knew her too well and had not forgotten that she also had a very healthy libido. After a while of just enjoying the feeling of her body against him, he bent down and kissed her on her forehead, stroking her golden, blonde hair that was so familiar to him. Again, she didn't pull away, and he knew for sure that she also wanted him. When he could postpone the moment no longer, he stood and took her hands, inviting her to stand, and they stood in front of each other looking into each other's eyes. He leaned forward and kissed her gently on the lips. Still she didn't pull away.

"What are you doing?" she asked in mock disbelief.

"I am allowing my body to do what it wants to and telling my mind to be quiet and sit quietly in a corner!"

He kissed her again. This time more fully, and her lips yielded a little and softened.

"Darling, I can't pretend that I know what I am doing, but I am pretty sure that what I feel for you is not just lust. It seems crazy, but even after all this time I still want to be with you," he said with a bashful look.

He told her of how he was not the same man that she had left three months before. Of how he had traveled a powerful journey through grief and loss to arrive at a place where he felt so much more at peace with himself. From what she had shared, he knew she had been conscious of doing her inner work, too.

"I have never felt so much for a woman before. All the crazy, beautiful magic that has happened between us! And you are here now, and I know that I still want you, so maybe we are not done yet?"

He felt that perhaps they had weathered the challenging storms and could now enjoy some calm sailing.

He didn't really know what he was saying. Was he just saying this because his desire for her was so intense, or was this something deeper than desire?

Despite everything that had happened, he still wanted to be with her. He knew they would need to do things differently, but he wanted to try again, to begin from a fresh, new, clean place. He didn't want to live the rest of his life wondering if they could have made it work if they had just had the courage to try once more.

She moved away from him and looked out of the window for what seemed like an eternity. Then, she turned to him.

She admitted that what he spoke of had also crossed her mind.

"Maybe I am crazy, too, but I know that I still want you in my life," she said simply.

She came close to him, and they kissed fully and deeply. His strong arms held her tightly, and his hands wasted no time as they stroked and caressed her Goddess-like form which he had missed so much. He pulled his mouth from hers and breathed her fragrance in a while, his open mouth tasted the soft flesh of her neck. She tasted more delicious than he had dared to remember and soon her arms were up in the air as he pulled her top over her head to reveal the pale flesh of her chest, gentle belly and delicate lace of her black bra. He was crazy with wanton desire for her, and she responded beautifully to his touch as she relaxed and surrendered to the energy and passion that engulfed them. Soft moans began to emanate from her lips, and this only aroused him more. The sound of her rising sensual ecstasy and joy as she surrendered to his attention was alluring music to his ears.

Soon, they were both naked, and she pushed him down into the armchair and parted his thighs. She knelt down and looked up, their eyes met, and love poured out and engulfed them. Then, she bent her head and took him deep into her hot, wet mouth. He gasped and moaned as she expertly ravaged him until he whimpered from the new level of sensation of an expertly administered fusion of pleasure and pain. As he looked down at her head rising and falling and the arch of her beautiful, elegant back, he was filled with gratitude for the moment.

When she was satisfied and finished, he thanked her with rough, passionate kisses. He could taste and smell himself on her saliva that glistened around her mouth. He led her to the bedroom where she lay on her back on the bed expectantly. He gently parted her thighs a little more so that she was open for him. God, how he had missed her. He savoured the moment; for a few seconds, she lay vulnerable and naked, waiting with anticipation knowing that soon she would have what she wanted. She would have the man inside her who wanted and loved and desired her so fully.

She was so very wet that he slipped easily inside. He held her wrists above her head with one hand and with the other hand he roughly fondled a breast with its erect, pert nipple. His mouth and tongue gave their full attention to her other breast while he slid again and again and again into the juicy wetness of her sacred depths. He was aware that he was wild and rough, but he was so hungry for her; perhaps he was punishing her a little for leaving him, too. Yes, he was punishing her with his desire and passion. He wanted to make love to her so fully and wonderfully, that she would never leave him again and never want to be made love to by another man.

The intensely charged energy between them rose and rose until he paused, laying quietly on her for a while kissing her face all over tenderly while he remained motionlessly inside her. Sometimes he would feel himself soften inside her and yet the energy being conducted between them would continue. Sometimes her body would convulse gently, at other times his back would arch as the waves of bliss traveled up his spine. And then the crescendo would rise again with their writhing bodies, slippery with sweat and saliva and white liquid fire. She moaned and gasped and screamed with delight and the sounds activated him more and more as they rose higher and higher and higher. And then his body would relax and soften, and they would lay together breathing as he remained motionless inside her again, his hands and mouth gently caressing her. Then the energy would rise once more. When he could contain himself no longer, he began to force himself harder and deeper inside her until they both climaxed in an explosion of ecstatic bliss together.

They lay in the gentle glow of softening passion; his chest rising and falling violently as his lungs desperately tried to take in enough oxygen to his exhausted and spent muscles. She stroked his long hair from his sweat-drenched face and kissed him gently over and over again.

Concerned that he might be squashing her with his relaxed weight, he mustered enough energy to slide off her. He kissed her soft glistening belly, and they lay side by side, floating in the magical energy that engulfed them. His mind was so very still, and he was totally at peace.

As he lay suspended in the sweetness, unexpected laughter began to rise up from deep inside him. This had happened sometimes before. As always, there were no thoughts attached to it, no reason for laughing, and yet he laughed. This time it was more violent; he laughed and laughed until tears were rolling down his cheeks. He was shrieking and writhing, and his stomach muscles hurt.

She was used to these laughing episodes and knew that every time she commented or said something it just made him laugh more. So she just waited it out quietly. Maybe the lovemaking had released some trapped energy, and it was something to do with kundalini, but he never concerned himself too much about it. Why would he? He was laughing, he was happy, and he was very much alive! After ten minutes or so the laughter subsided, and he rolled onto his side, snuggling up to her under the warm cosiness of the duvet.

They talked long into the night, and she shared the new elements of her powerful spiritual journey that had continued to unfold after they had parted. She had continued to have unusual experiences, and her stories endeared her to him even more. He listened, hopeful that since he had let go of so much neediness and pain in their time apart, and that she had been doing her inner work, too, that there really was a possibility that things would be calmer and sweeter between them. Perhaps they could make it work. They talked about how they needed to do things differently, and she promised that she would do her best to be more open, honest and vulnerable.

They both knew only too well how a conscious relationship would bring any unresolved trauma and issues to the surface, but how much more could there possibly be? There were no guarantees that they would grow old together, this was now an idea that he had already let go of. It was enough that she was here with him now.

He began to caress her soft womanly flesh and soon the sexual energy was coursing through his body again. In the three months that they had been apart, he had shared his bed a few times with other women, but these experiences had been like trying to satiate a fierce thirst by eating snow. The deep intimacy and connection that he felt with her had not been present; his attempts to delete it from his memory had only made him more aware of how their lovemaking had always been out of this world. In comparison to the others, she was like a cool mountain spring on a scorching hot day. They drank from each other as they made love again, but this time it was a gentle, tender dance. When they were finally complete in their enjoyment of each other they settled down to get some sleep as the gentle grey light of dawn began to creep around the bedroom blinds.

As he lay listening to the familiar steady rhythm of her sleeping breath beside him, he made himself a promise. He knew that so many of the challenges that they had faced were because of his fear of opening fully to her and loving her unconditionally, just the way she was. So, he pledged, as he lay there, that he would place no future expectations on their time together. When he was with her, he would enjoy her companionship, her kindness, her sparkly character, her beauty, and her sexiness. When they were not together, he would continue with his life, as he had become accustomed to, while they had been separated. It seemed so simple, but what he didn't see was that even though he was taking responsibility for his part in their previous challenges, in attempting to make things work better between them, he was still grasping onto a future for them. This was a sign that he was either still fearful of losing her or still fearful of being alone; maybe it's just what you do when you are with your twin flame!

As soon as he awoke, he felt uneasy and sad, knowing that they both had their lives to attend to. This was the reality, regardless of how much he just wanted to stay in bed with her all day. As had always been the way, it never felt as if there was enough time for them. He walked her to her car outside, and they held each other tightly under the soft white sky. He desperately wanted to ask when he could see her again, but he decided that he would refrain from this. He was turning over a new leaf, so instead, he closed the car door behind her.

"I will be in touch," he said as casually as he could, through the open car window.

She smiled and drove away. He stood on the drive, just feeling his breath and watching the birds. After a while, he made his way up the drive and back down the steps into his flat.

CHAPTER 16

He was determined that this time it would be different. Gone was his obsession with needing to have a future with her. From now on he was focusing on a future with himself. He would continue taking care of himself to nurture and heal the twin flame union of masculine and feminine within him. He had come to see how she had been showing him all the places that he was not loving himself. He saw that when he looked outside himself to her to compensate for his inner lack, things became fraught and challenging. Through his work to continue honouring the divine feminine within, he was becoming more complete unto himself. He was deepening into his sacred masculinity. His time in nature fed his need for intimacy with the feminine, as did the sweet mantras sung by female vocalists. He was being the mother to himself that he had never really had, and this was bringing him home; home to the divine union within his tender heart.

In between their time together he did as he had planned and just got on with his life. His focus on his mission in the world was gathering energy all the time, and he had begun a new project giving talks in schools about his life story. He shared how there are gifts in adversity and that success is not just dependent on what happens, but on how we choose to respond to what happens. He wanted to inspire young people and give them hope because he felt that it was a particularly challenging time to be growing up. He jokingly saw himself as a selfish altruist because he knew that by helping and empowering the youth, he was also serving himself. Apart from when he was with her, he felt most alive when he was helping others.

He purposely didn't message her very often because he was aware that he didn't want his time to be spent waiting for her reply as he had so often done before. He wanted to break the pattern and forget about her as much as possible when they were apart. He didn't want his life to be a continuous flow of waiting for the next morsel of connection from her or the next banquet when they could allow their naked bodies to merge in the magical realms of the bedroom.

Though his mind crept in at times and his critical thought patterns and neediness began to emerge, this time he was more alert. He would catch the thoughts more quickly, and the intensity of his neediness was greatly diminished. He kept reminding himself that they would walk together for as long as it served them both.

Things had changed at the café, and she had even less time for their meetings at weekends. Since they had been apart, she had busied herself deepening her connection with her girlfriends, and she had plenty of social events already planned for the coming weekends in her diary. He resigned himself to this and saw it as an opportunity to keep deepening his love and acceptance of himself in the free time that he had when he was not busy with work. He spent more time with his friends and consciously invested more energy in his relationship with his eldest sister.

Work on the book about them ground to a halt, the words just wouldn't flow. Somehow it didn't feel right to be focusing so much on the past. Plus, it was a story that had once come to an end, but now it was clearly not yet over. He resigned himself to putting it on hold. Occasionally, it was mentioned in conversation, and although she was more comfortable with the idea of their story being in print than she had been initially, it was clear that she still found the idea difficult. At times it felt a bit like the elephant in the room but, as he knew that he had to write their story, he decided that there was really nothing to gain in talking about it and it was mentioned less and less.

His walks on the hills became a deeper and deeper spiritual practise, and he saw clearly that his time with Mother Earth fed and facilitated his longing to reconnect fully with the divine feminine within him. He would often remove his shoes as soon as he got onto the ridge and sigh inwardly at the feel of the warm, soft mossy grass. On other parts of the walk, he relished the cold firmness of the granite protrusions underfoot as he made his way higher and higher up and along the ridge until his outstretched arms felt that they could almost touch the clouds skimming by in the vast expanse of sky. The grass and the rock reminded him of his life's journey: sometimes things were hard, and sometimes things were soft. The contrast brought a richness and perspective to the whole experience.

On the ridge, his spirit felt wild and free and, like the buzzards that joined him, the higher vision from his vantage point always eased any fears or concerns that his mind had been burdening him with. When the conditions were right, he would stand and face the windy gusts and allow his long hair to be blown and billowed like a ragged sail. It felt awesome. Sometimes a great sense of peace would descend upon him as he stood, motionless. He would feel the sweetness of existence with his closed eyes and, inhaling and exhaling deeply, a profound sense of gratitude for being blessed with the gift of life would engulf him. Sometimes, he couldn't contain all the feelings, and his eyes would leak tears that rolled down his face and fall onto the waiting earth.

He saw how he had still been looking outwardly to this beautiful woman to meet a need, to heal a wound that could only be healed within himself. She would never fill the longing that was his constant companion because, in truth, it was not really a longing for her, but a longing for himself. He now deeply desired the feminine aspect of himself that he had banished from his life so many years before. And he knew that he was also a man and that his desire for a woman was not to be denied or to cause shame, because sexual energy is indeed the energy of creation and life itself. This truth began to flow potently through him. Life had orchestrated the perfect conditions and, with her help, he was being cleared out of fear and the last remnant of wounding. He had traveled so far down this road with her help, and he felt profoundly indebted.

They met up every now and again, and when he was not with her, he found that he was more able to be fully present with himself. The longing for her was gentler. There was a honeymoon period of a few weeks, but as the weeks merged into months of the new chapter of their togetherness, it became increasingly clear to them that the catalytic healing power of their combined energy was not done with them yet. And so, a new dynamic began to emerge.

It seemed that although there were not so many physical kundalini experiences taking place in her body, the clearing energy was working its magic. Before their separation, it seemed to be primarily his fear and wounding that was arising. Now, a wave of her own deep wounds began to take center stage and show themselves for the light of consciousness to transform.

The bigger current picture of her life was far from ideal, and she still had challenges taking place regularly with her family. Her financial situation was not easy, and the menopausal symptoms only added to the weight upon her shoulders. He could see how there were things that she was doing that were not making life easy for herself, and how fear was clouding her judgment. She was such a proud creature, and he had learned that she would take his concern and suggestions as criticism and withdraw from him if he shared his thoughts. So, he learned to keep his perspective to himself, for the most part, seeing it as an opportunity not to be a rescuer, but rather to deepen his faith that she would see what she was ready to see when the time was right. But, as a result of her current situation, when she finally arrived at his flat so that they could have some time together, she would invariably be depleted, exhausted and emotional.

Sometimes, she would unexpectedly snap at him and withdraw. On the surface, there seemed to be no apparent reason. But he knew well that her emotional response was the result of her tiredness and triggering of her own wounds. He would do his very best to remain centered and not take her words or actions personally, even though he still felt uncomfortable when she withdrew behind her icy defenses. But the degree of abandonment that he felt now was so much less; often, he would not react at all, choosing instead to wait until she was ready to return to him with his open arms and heart.

Other times, he did not manage to remain calm, and his own fear would be triggered, leading him to lash out with words that only resulted in her withdrawing for longer. He began to see more clearly that the more that he could remain centered and open, the safer that she would feel. He didn't really need to say anything, he just needed to listen with his heart. If she projected stuff onto him, all he had to do was allow it to slide off him like water from a ducks' back. When she felt safe and heard the storm inside begin to subside, once again there would be the closeness and intimacy between them that was his heart's desire.

ONE SUNDAY AFTERNOON they were lying on the bed in his flat. She was particularly tired, due in large part to a recent bereavement in the family. The stress of the loss, and organizing the funeral, had taken its toll, and she hadn't been sleeping much.

She began to tell him again about the financial challenges that she was facing, and he tried his best just to listen and hold space for her. But it was so hard because it felt like she was moaning and complaining about a situation that he had heard so many times already. He could see that her fear was blinding her to the course of action that would bring an end to the suffering that she was experiencing. Her lack of self-worth seemed to be being directly mirrored by the flow of abundance in her life. He could see this, but she wasn't ready to see it herself. He could see how beautiful she was and how worthy she was of an easy, flowing, abundant life, but she was oblivious as to how she was blocking the flow.

He had spoken many times about them living together, knowing that one of the benefits would be an easing of the financial pressure on both of them, but she had never seemed very open to this. She was still so nervous about arguments and heated conversation or raised voices, which she assumed would be more frequent if they lived together. She found the whole idea unsettling, yet for him, cohabiting was a natural progression of a relationship. He so wanted to be able to take care of her. As his financial income was steadily increasing, they could live very comfortably if they shared a home.

One evening, when he was feeling brave, he had asked her if she was willing to commit to meeting up for an evening in the week, as well as on weekends. The expression on her face was very telling, and when he asked her what feeling had arisen in response to his question, she responded honestly and vulnerably that the question had evoked fear in her.

In that moment he knew that there was no future for them, as far as a traditional monogamous relationship was concerned. He chided himself for not being content with the present and trying to engineer a future again together. It seemed as if there was no way of the connection deepening if they could not even commit to spending more time in each other's company. They were spending less time together now than they were before the breakup. Though he felt so much for her, he began to see that, although on some level she cared about him, her fear was just too great to give herself more fully to him. The awareness evoked a sharp stabbing pain in his solar plexus, and he pushed it away, and the incident was soon forgotten.

CHAPTER 17

The sky was mottled with scruffy clouds, and the spring sun was doing its best to warm the air. They were sat on the hill in their special spot surrounded by the remnants of a picnic and nature's beauty, but all was not well. As he listened to her complaining again about an issue that she had with one of her siblings, he just couldn't keep his mouth shut and the smart ass, mister fix-it in him, as gently as possible, offered her a solution to her situation. She physically pulled away from him, and the petulant girl in her snapped at him for his inability to just listen and hear her. She began to get up and walk away.

"Please don't go, honey," he pleaded as he grabbed her wrist. She slapped his hand away and stormed off across the greenery, turning briefly to hurl some accusations in his direction.

He lay down for a while on the soft green grass and told himself that everything was fine, that she would soon return. However, the minutes crept by and soon an hour had passed. He tidied up the picnic and returned everything to the car and set out over the hills to look for her. He could feel a sense of panic rising in him; as usual, he was concerned that their short and precious time together would be over if he couldn't find her. Even if he could find her on the hills, he might not be able to reach her behind her cold, protective wall.

There were so many paths that she could have walked on and soon he gave up the hopeless task. He made his way back to the car, hoping that she might be there waiting for him. A couple of hours had passed by this time, and he thought it was possible that she might have walked back home, so he got in the car and drove. He did not pass her on the road or find her at his flat when he got there.

He turned around and got back into the car. He knew that she was tired and that the walk back would be tough for her, so he set off back up the hill. He was angry with her for leaving him again and yet, at the same time, he felt deep compassion for her; she had so much on her plate. He knew that when he found her, he needed to be calm and kind.

To his delight, he saw her walking along the road, and he pulled over and leaned across to open the door.

"Get in," he said in a soft, kind voice.

They drove back in silence, and he left her in the living room while he lay on the bed to center himself. He was just pleased that they were in the same space and was optimistic that the little drama could soon be put behind them.

Before long she came into the bedroom and sat at the end of the bed. She apologised and told him how blown away she was that he had come back to find her even though her behaviour had been so outrageous. She told him of how she was not proud of how she had behaved, but that she had just found a quiet place on the hill and had fallen asleep.

He, in turn, told her calmly about how worried he had been and soon she was in his arms, and he was stroking her golden hair tenderly. He felt so much for her that it was easy to forgive her. They decided to watch a movie and soon they were snuggled together on the bed with the laptop, while outside the light began to fade.

It had been two months since they had got back together, and even though he tried as best as he could to just go with the flow, an increasing number of fear-based thoughts precipitated a rising tension in him. The old, familiar feeling that he was walking on eggshells grew and grew. She was exhausted, and all sorts of memories and painful emotions from her childhood were rising to the surface. She was wobbling and buckling under the weight of life's challenges; they were coming too fast, and there was never time to regroup, to find a solid footing and rest fully before the next emotional storm wave had arisen to take its toll on her depleted energy.

He did what he could to support her, and she did her best to open up and allow herself to be vulnerable. Sometimes, though, his impatience and frustration got the better of him, and he would not listen as well as he could. Instead, he would offer solutions that she was not ready to hear. They had even less time together these days to go through the storm and find the learning or the gift in what had arisen so that they might sink back into deep connection and a warm, loving space of togetherness. If they were lucky, they would find a degree of reconciliation, but there was rarely complete closure on the issues that arose. All too often their work and family obligations took priority and caused them to have days apart with no communication. By the time they came back together, her fear of vulnerable communication meant that she seldom wanted to carry on where they had left off. Though he knew that leaving feelings unexpressed and words unsaid were dangerous, he just couldn't see a solution.

It became clear to him that their time together was coming to an end again, and he did his best to accept the inevitable. The 'if only' thoughts kept him hanging on, and occasionally he entertained the idea of walking away, but he just couldn't bring himself to leave her. He knew in his heart that every moment with this beautiful woman was a blessing.

Their last full weekend together was at her place. They had gone out into the city for the afternoon, and after having drinks at a quiet bar, they set off to find somewhere to eat. It was early, and there was a selection of restaurants to choose from on the busy street in the Indian area of the city. She had been particularly negative and moody all day, and he kept reminding himself that she was tired, that he didn't need to take it personally. She took ages to decide which restaurant she was happy with. His legs were tired from walking the hard pavements in his smart shoes, and his hunger was severely impacting his patience.

While they sat at the table waiting for the waiter, she spoke about the book that she was currently reading about kundalini energy and the awakening of consciousness. He found himself a little distracted by an argument going on between a couple at the other side of the restaurant. She rolled her eyes, and he apologised. She continued talking, and he did his best to focus while the alcohol from the second beer he was drinking went straight to his head; he rarely drank alcohol anymore, especially on an empty stomach.

A waitress walked past, and he noted her short skirt and revealingly tight blouse.

"I don't appreciate you looking that woman up and down while I am talking to you," she said sharply.

He did his best to explain that he noticed everyone that walked by; he had just noticed the waitress in the same way.

"It's quite natural for a man to be aware of attractive women, but you should know by now that I only have feelings for you."

"Well, I don't appreciate it. I saw how you looked at her."

"How did I look at her?" he asked. He admitted that he had noticed that she was attractive and that she was revealing quite a lot of her chest.

"I don't appreciate it," she repeated. "How do you think that feels for me?"

The alcohol had loosened his tongue. The full frustration at her behaviour and moodiness all day got the better of him, and he raised his voice at her.

"Look, if you have issues about aging and younger women, don't project that onto me. Yes, I did notice the attractive waitress, but it was nothing more than that."

"Don't raise your voice at me," she retorted. "I know what I saw."

"I've had enough of you for one day," he said. "I am getting a taxi. I'll see you back at your place."

He shot her a look of disgust and stormed out of the restaurant.

Back at her place, he lay on the bed, feeling wretched. How was he back in this place again? How dare she? It seemed like she always had to be right. After everything he had put up with all day from her, this really was the last straw.

Eventually, she returned and though he had tried his best to let all his anger go, the moment she walked in the door he gave her the full force of all his pent-up sense of injustice. She recoiled in alarm at the fierceness of his emotional onslaught. He became more and more frustrated by her insistence that the incident in the bar was nothing to do with her own insecurity. He didn't agree. At one point, she tried to leave the bedroom, saying that she was going to sleep on the sofa. He took her wrists and made her face him, speaking quietly, but firmly to her. "Darling, I just don't think you are seeing things clearly. You have so much on your plate now, you are tired, and you have been in a bad mood all day."

"Let go of me," she said.

He did, immediately horrified that he had allowed his anger to make him behave in such an uncharacteristic way.

Distraught and defeated, he turned away and collapsed onto her bed. He allowed the feelings of exasperation to wash over him until he fell asleep, alone.

When they woke up, they started arguing almost where they had left off the night before, although this time he conceded that there may have been some lust in his eyes when he had looked at the waitress. They had been so disconnected of late, and he knew that in the past a sure sign that a relationship was in danger was when his attention began to wander. They saw so little of each other now, and when they were together, she was often tired or distant or both. He knew that it was possible that she may have been right about how he had looked at the waitress. He apologised half-heartedly, but soon they were talking about how it really didn't seem to be working between them.

There were many things about their relationship that were different this time. However, as they talked, it seemed clear to him that she had given up but didn't want to be the one to admit that it was over. The conversation was a subtle dance of honesty and dishonesty, as neither wanted to be the first to say the words that are so hard to return from, especially since they had already tried once before. They both knew that if it came to an end this time there really would be no going back.

After a time, he plucked up the courage and said the inevitable. "We seem to be saying that we can't see a way back from here and that this isn't working. Would you agree?" he sighed.

She seldom gave a direct reply and this time was no different. He had often said in a semi-joking way that her ability to not respond directly to a question would have made her a great politician.

She stalled and avoided answering the question directly for a while, but when he pushed her, she conceded that it didn't seem to be working.

The realisation of what was happening hit them both, and there was a softening. They sat together for a while and talked more gently to each other about how they wished things could have been different. They both began to own their part in the reasons for this imminent parting.

He packed his stuff into his bag, and she walked him to the door of her home. They hugged and thanked each other for everything they had learned, the beauty they had shared and the numerous other gifts that had been exchanged. They looked each other in the eyes for a moment and then he turned away and wandered down the path to where his car waited.

He didn't know why, but the thought that kept running through his mind as he drove along the familiar roads was 'How is it that we never seem to know when the last time will be that we will make love to the person that we love so much?'

He knew in his heart that it was over. He knew that they had tried so hard, no one was really to blame. It just wasn't meant to be. As the car made its way home, he decided to let her go gracefully, and he knew that he would be fine. They had come to the end of the road, and now it was time to get on with the next chapter of his life.

It was still early when he got home, but he was tired and drained from the short, broken night of sleep. After a long soak in the bath with some lavender oil, he put himself to bed. He lay in the quietness and missed her but was acutely aware that his grief was much softer and gentler than it had been previously. Soon, he had drifted off to sleep.

CHAPTER 18

He awoke in his bed, alone and disoriented. Then the realisation of what had been decided the following day came flooding back, and he lay for a while, allowing the information to wash over him. And then he noticed it. Something unexpected had happened, or rather, had not happened. There were none of the familiar sensations in his body that he had become so accustomed to when she had stonewalled him or when the relationship had ended before. Although he felt a gentle sadness knowing that they would not lie together again, there was no nausea, no sinking feeling in his stomach, no dull ache in the chest. He still had an appetite.

He smiled to himself as he realised that this was another aspect of her bringing him home. She had brought him home to the present. He could clearly feel some grief and sadness as a low vibration, but this time he barely felt any real physical discomfort. No longer was his body full of trauma from his childhood. The challenges that she had gifted him had been an opportunity to purge, to release and delete some old timelines that had previously always connected any relationship with a woman to the brief relationship that he had had with his mother. From the warmth of his bed, he sent blessings and gratitude to the beautiful woman who had been such a powerful instrument of grace and healing for him. He had suspected that their meeting had been divinely orchestrated, but now he was without a doubt.

There was a gentle grief that permeated his days for a while. It was most difficult when the weekends arrived, and he had space that normally would have been filled by their togetherness. But he knew deep down that they now had separate paths to walk. He knew that she had a tough road ahead of her. He wished that he could have been there to travel with her, but this was obviously not meant to be. He knew that he would be just fine. Now was an opportunity to deepen his self-love and acceptance even more and, in so doing, tend to his own inner marriage and deepen further into his sacred masculinity.

Still, he missed her. Even though they had decided that they would remain friends and occasionally spoke on the phone or messaged each other a little, he missed their intimacy. It was good to connect with her, but he noticed that it was hard to see her just as a friend when they had up until recently been such ardent lovers. He got a little too excited, then, when a message arrived from her. The anticipation of her responding started to increase in intensity, too. Perhaps he had not really moved on to the extent that he hoped, emotionally or mentally, and there was still a part of him that had not accepted that it was over.

After a few weeks, he could no longer deny the truth that he was longing to make love to her again. 'Just one more time' he told himself; 'just give me one more night.' No matter how hard he tried to avoid the thought, it kept coming back!

A few months earlier, she had surprised him with a lovely birthday celebration meal. One of the many thoughtful presents she bought him were some tickets to go to a bird of prey center where he could actually fly some of the magnificent hunter birds that he felt such an affinity with.

On the day before he was due to go, he was feeling somewhat disconsolate that he would have to go alone with no one to take photos of him and the birds. He had tried to think of a friend who might go with him, but the few that he called the week before were either at work or had other plans. He guessed that everyone else in the group would be with their partner or a friend and he would be by himself.

And then her message arrived, wishing him a lovely time with the birds. He liked to think that part of the reason that she got in touch was because she hoped that he might invite her. The tickets had been bought to go on a Monday when she would not be at work in the café, so he knew that there would be a good chance that she was free to come. Before he could really think too much about what he was doing, he had responded to her message and asked her if she would like to join him.

In her usual way, she said she needed time to think about it, but he didn't have to wait too long. After a couple of hours, she replied in the affirmative. His heart skipped a beat knowing that once again he would be with this amazing woman who had turned his world upside down through an incredible journey of healing and love. Again, the image of the moth and the flame came to mind, and he knew that he should probably not see her if he was ever going to lay his feelings to rest completely. The thought of her naked in his bed still had a powerful hold on him, though. His intuition told him that she was also not finding it easy to let him go and that this was what lay behind her initial innocent message to him.

SHE ARRIVED AT his place looking as radiant as ever in a pretty blouse, long cotton, Indian style skirt, and sandals. He could see that she was tired, but that did not detract from her beauty. The sun was already warm, and it promised to be a beautiful English summer's day. They set off in his car, and he quickly noticed that it felt as if they had never really broken up. It was like they were just a regular couple off on a day trip together. As he drove down windy lanes with bushy hedges and patchwork fields, the conversation was light and easy, and they laughed a lot.

The experience with the birds was wonderful. He handled an array of magnificent creatures and loved when they flew to the thick leather glove on his hand to claim their prize of morsels of fresh meat. The eagle owl was probably the most impressive, especially when it sat nonchalantly on the glove and looked straight into his eyes for quite a while as if they were old friends.

As they drove away down the bumpy track, he thanked her profusely for her lovely birthday gift, adding that it was vastly improved by her presence. She had also taken lots of photographs which he was keen to look at on the computer when he got home.

But, of course, something else had been at the back of his mind. Now that they were driving in the direction of home, he knew clearly that he did not want to say goodbye yet. He asked if she was hungry and offered to buy them lunch at a pub he liked. It was in a picturesque setting by the river on route. She protested feebly that it might not be a good idea because of emotional entanglements and such, but when he pressed a little, she quite easily gave in and agreed to accept the invitation.

Although he wasn't a vegetarian, he didn't usually eat red meat, but today he ordered a beef burger and chips because he felt like he needed something that would really ground him. He was feeling rather nervous because he knew that at some point he was going to have to try and find the best way to ask her to stay with him overnight. They ate outside, and when she had finished her vegetable curry, they sat on the grass by the meandering river with their drinks.

It seemed clear to him from her body language that she would be open to his suggestion. Behind the façade of their light-hearted banter, he was preparing himself for the crucial moment, while at the same time bracing himself for the possible sense of disappointment and rejection. She still looked so beautiful in his eyes, and as they sat on the grass, just a few inches of thigh or a glimpse of flesh between the buttons of her blouse was enough to make his heart flutter with passion and desire.

At one point, she lay back on the ground with her hands behind her head and instinctively he seized the moment and bent over quickly to give her a swift kiss on her lips.

"What are you doing?" she asked, with what seemed to him like mock surprise.

He laughed. "Darling, I think we have been here before."

He knew that she still had feelings for him. She probably wanted him as much as he wanted her.

"I know it's crazy, but perhaps we have just one more chance, one more opportunity to make love before we say goodbye properly."

She looked at him intensely. "Well, I might be able to be persuaded, but don't you think it might just confuse everything, having to say goodbye all over again?"

He knew that she was probably right, it would be upsetting, but the following morning seemed like a lifetime away. He had never been one for playing things safe. He was more than willing to throw caution to the wind for one more night of passion with her.

He spoke honestly in response to what she had said, as the excitement began to grow in his body. He told her how hungry he was for her and that there would be no strings attached. After all, they were both grown-ups. It was entirely up to them what they decided to do.

"Any other concerns you might want to share?" he asked, feeling confident enough now to be a little sarcastic.

"No," she said reaching over and slapping his thigh playfully. "But" she added with a serious look on her face, "If we are to make love one last time, I have a condition."

He knew that it was very unlikely that he would not agree to her condition, but he was a little apprehensive.

"Tell me, what is your condition?"

"I want you to make love to me on the earth. Take me somewhere where we can lie on the ground and where the sky will be the only roof over us."

He grinned much too much, knowing that his dream of being naked with her again was coming true. He loved her idea of their last time together being held in the arms of mother earth. It was an easy condition to agree to.

But he couldn't think of anywhere that they could go where they were sure not to be disturbed in their last precious moments of lovemaking. He asked if she might not prefer the comfort of his bed, but she was adamant that it had to be somewhere out in nature. He gazed into the river that carelessly flowed along at the bottom of the bank and settled his mind a little. Then, as he had hoped it would, an idea arrived. They would go to the place where he had taken her many months before on his birthday. The old oak tree would be the only witness, as the field was quite secluded, and it was highly unlikely that any dog walkers would be out since daylight was fading already. He was a happy man, and he thanked her for having such a wonderful, ridiculously romantic idea.

As they drove towards their destination, the excitement in his chest was almost too much to bear. To make things worse, or better, she reached over and undid the belt and then the button and then the zip on his jeans. She proceeded to fondle him tenderly while he tried his best to concentrate on the road.

"You know honey, there have been so many times when I wanted to ask you to do this for me while we were driving, but for some reason I never did."

"Well, that's funny because there were so many times when I wanted to but didn't feel brave enough," she coyly replied.

The irony of the situation hit him, and he thought of all the other times when they had probably not been honest or vulnerable enough with each other in expressing their needs or wants. How many missed opportunities had there been for pleasure or expressing themselves or sharing something that instead had just remained a secret thought?

He parked the car in the small layby and took his coat from the back seat. They made their way hand in hand across a couple of fields to a quiet, secluded spot where the grass gave way to some ancient woodland. They looked about for a spot where the land was reasonably level, and there weren't too many thistles or nettles. Soon they agreed on a small natural indent in the ground. This was to be the sacred spot where they would make love together one last time. The ancient oak tree stood a modest distance away and took no notice of them.

The air was beginning to cool a little as the sun had long gone and they wasted no time in allowing their bodies to come together. She was always so beautiful to kiss; their lips and tongues met enthusiastically like old, reunited friends. There was no inhibition or shyness, just a genuine, honest passion and desire to be together. They undressed unceremoniously, throwing their clothes untidily on the floor around the coat and, in no time at all, she was where he loved her best, on her back, naked with her thighs apart.

Their brief, but passionate foreplay had worked it's magic and, as always, she was easy for him to enter. The natural setting seemed to awaken a little of the wild man in him, and he enjoyed the firmness of the earth under her back. There was no yielding of a mattress which allowed him to push harder and deeper inside her than usual. She made her sounds of pleasure while the gentle breeze caressed the trees and the leaves whispered of their own delight at the wind's attention.

The slightly damp earth smelt pungent and strong and mixed with the smell of the delicious juice that emanated from between her soft thighs. He saw the sky and clouds reflected in her eyes as the dance of their lovemaking rose and fell. The sounds of her joy as she orgasmed soon brought him to a sweet, transcendent climax as well. Once he was no longer inside her, he kissed her, one last time, tenderly on her soft, white belly. They lay side by side on the earth, looking up into the heavens and feeling the cool air on their passion-warmed flesh. She moved the coat that she lay on a little so that that the combined mixture of their sacred elixir trickled from her directly onto the earth.

He thanked her, and she thanked him, and there was nothing else to say. The last of the daylight was fast beginning to disappear, and she shivered, despite his attempt at keeping her warm by arranging their bundle of clothes on top of her. They dressed in silence and made their way back to the car as the new crescent moon showed herself above the tree line on the ridge in a brief clearing that appeared in the cloudy sky. He felt a slight pang in his chest as he remembered that this really was their last time. But he dismissed the thought and brought his attention back to their last moments together.

On arriving back at his place, she came in to use the toilet, and they shared a cup of tea and talked about things that really didn't matter. It was as if they were both prolonging the inevitable. But soon the pressures of time meant that once again he was walking her to her car. They embraced once again and thanked each other for everything that they had shared. She got into her little green car and drove away.

As HE TIDIED up his flat in the morning, he came upon her scarf underneath his coat. He messaged her and teased, suggesting that she had left it on purpose so that she would have an excuse to return. They had spoken clearly about not seeing each other again so that they could both move on and proceed with their separate lives. They had meant it, but he began to wonder whether life had other plans.

As the day progressed, though, he realised that he needed to end their connection properly. There was still a part of him that belonged to her, and he didn't want it to be this way anymore. It wasn't fair to him or her; it didn't feel right. They couldn't keep stopping and starting, and he knew that at some point they would have to cut the connection cleanly once and for all.

After all, he had gotten his wish. They had made love one more time, and how amazing and beautiful and special it had been. How divine, how precious, how fitting to end their incredible journey in such a way.

He was aware that with her, as in all of his relationships, he had always waited for the woman to decide when it was over. This time he needed to do it differently. He needed to be the one to say clearly that they had come to the end of the road. In doing so, he would be making a clear statement that he was no longer afraid to be alone. Finally, he was at peace with himself. He no longer needed a woman to make him feel complete.

He picked up her scarf and held it to his face so that he could breathe her fragrance in, and then he packed it into a jiffy bag and wrote her address on it. He added a £10.00 note to the parcel with a short message explaining that the money was a symbol of all the financial abundance that was going to come her way from unexpected, as well as expected, places. The package was sealed with a loving kiss.

He walked the short distance through the park into town and up to the post office with the small parcel in his hand. It was light, but it felt heavy. He knew that once he had posted this, there was no going back. No more 'just one more lovemaking,' no more waiting for an opportunity to message her or see her. This was it. This really was the end.

The lady behind the counter at the Post Office was blissfully unaware of the gravity of the service she was providing, and he watched as his innocent little package disappeared into a sack behind the counter.

He made his way back through the town while the world around him carried on, oblivious to what had just transpired. The birds carried on singing, and the clouds carried on drifting, and the world carried on spinning.

His legs felt clumsy, but there was a smile on his face. He had done it. He had let her go of his own volition. His heart was filled with gratitude for all that they had shared, and he knew, he knew without a shadow of a doubt, that she had done what had been asked. He was home. He was at peace.

Back at his flat he poured himself a glass of water, lit a candle, and placed them on the desk. Muttering a prayer under his breath, he pulled the open laptop towards him. He gazed out of the window while it loaded up and took a few deep breaths.

After all, he was a writer, and he had a book to write, now that he knew how the story ended. As usual, his fingers hovered for a moment above the keys before dropping gently down to begin their clickety, staccato dance around the keyboard.

EPILOGUE

D o not be fooled by Her sweet, alluring smile, or lulled into a false sense of security by the kindness of Her gentle voice or the shy glances from Her pretty eyes.

She is a Siren and Her most precious gift to you will be to entice you on to the Ocean of Love, to set sail, innocently unaware of the hidden secrets beneath Her sometimes calm and sometimes tempestuous waters.

The delicious curves of Her Goddess like form will invite you to navigate the stormy waves of Her ruthless integrity while your destiny beckons you onto the jagged rocks of your own fear and cowardice.

And there, as you lie bleeding and desolate, the poison that lay blocked and trapped in the deepest place of your pierced heart will trickle forth and you shall be purged.

Your excruciating pain will ebb and flow to be dissolved in the infinite Ocean of Love while its salty water will both sting and cleanse your open wound.

And there will be deep and profound healing as your self-worth and honour return.

Battered and bloody, you shall crawl over the sharp rocks and then scramble to kinder ground to rest until you are ready to walk again;

Eventually, dried by the sun's rays and soothed by the cool breeze you will again stand; upright and proud, taller than you have ever been before. You shall make your way back to your rightful throne, that awaited you for so long, empty and neglected.

And as you feel into the unfamiliarity and unexpected peace of this new place you shall be filled with a vast sense of wonder and awe and humility at the power and magic of Her.

And yes, She too shall have her voyage, for though She is a Siren, She is a child, too. And there will be times when Her wounds will need dressing; wounds from the coarse tear of old, binding ropes.

Tend them with your strong, loving hands.

She too will need to be held softly and tenderly while old tears fall from Her weary eyes rising up from the depths of Her wounded heart.

She will need your patience and kindness; there will be no place for fear infused thoughts, words or actions.

And yet, She will test you time and time again to make sure you are worthy of entering the deepest places within Her sacred body and soul where holy treasures lie.

When you appear to fail, She may be ruthless at first, but Her kindness will grow as She learns to trust and forgive once again.

Your discernment will need to be sharp and true if you are to be clear of when to cut through the emotional tangled knots of Her past;

And to know when to speak from the depths of your sovereignty to pull Her from the waters of her own floundering self-doubt.

You must know when to guide Her, though at first, She will not be willing, addicted as She is to her own autonomy forged over years and years from the interminable weakness of previous lovers.

And you must know when to be guided by Her.

You must know when to listen softly and gently, holding Her hand tenderly or stroking Her silken hair while silencing the cacophony of voices in your head demanding you to advise or to fix or to mend.

Remember that She is your crystal clear mirror and that what you see in Her, is your Self.

What you forgive in Her is what you forgive in your Self.

She has come to destroy who you thought you were and to make you whole and your task is to gift Her the same treasure.

This new land will be beyond your wildest dreams.

Are you ready to be loved by a woman such as this?

Then lay down your weapons, for the rules of engagement here are nakedness, vulnerability, and deep, raw, honesty.

Your prize shall be a great peace within, and Love will flow through and into you in a way that your mind could never have begun to comprehend.

Set sail on the Ocean of Love and set your course for home.

THE END

ACKNOWLEDGMENTS

I would like to express my deep gratitude to every person that I have met so far in this lifetime. Whether family, friends, lovers or the briefest of encounters; you have all played an essential part in shaping my inner landscape and preparing me to write this book. Also, my thanks go to everyone at Sacred Stories Publishing, especially Evan and Patricia for being such awesome midwives in the birthing of this sacred story.

ABOUT THE AUTHOR

Miguel Dean was born in 1968 in Colchester, England. He had a challenging start to life which included the death of his mother from cancer when he was only seven months old. As a result of his early difficulties, as a young man, he spiraled down into a life of violence, petty crime, addiction, and homelessness in which he spent seven years living on the road as a New Age Traveler. It was the love of his newborn son that inspired and motivated him to begin to take responsibility and make changes. This was the beginning of a rich and varied and at times extremely challenging journey to return to healing and wholeness. Some of the more recent challenges that he faced and overcame include divorce, illness, and addiction. As a very experiential learner, Miguel was forced to develop a high sense of self-awareness which served him in setting his course and navigating his way home.

For the last twenty years, he has been immersed in the 'twin paths' of healing and transformation which can be summarized as an inner journey to heal his wounds, facilitated, and complemented by his contribution to the service of others and spiritually rooted social change. He worked for many years with the homeless before progressing into the education sector where he designed, wrote, and delivered courses to empower disadvantaged youth and the staff who worked with them. But eventually he became disillusioned with the constraints of the colleges where he worked, and for the last ten years, he has been immersed in the world of self-employment as an author, poet, speaker, and facilitator.

Miguel has now evolved into a profoundly effective catalyst for change in the marriage of the divine twin flame masculine and feminine within adults. His intuitive- sensitive nature and honest, authentic and open-heartedness are amongst the gifts he has to share. His writing and other offerings are in alignment with his passion for serving and easing the transition, from what no longer serves humanity and the planet, into a more beautiful world for our children and the generations to come.

www.migueldean.net